Early praise for *Simplifying JavaScript*

You should probably jot down each Tip from this book on Post-It notes and plaster them all over your desk area. These simple, practical bits of advice will have a profound effect on simplifying your JavaScript.

➤ **Kyle Simpson**
Author of *You Don't Know JS* and Open Web Evangelist

Joe provides a clear, organized path to mastering key JavaScript concepts. This isn't a boring textbook. It's a playbook filled with practical, real-world approaches to writing modular, maintainable, and modern JavaScript.

➤ **Cory House**
Pluralsight Author and International Speaker and Consultant, reactjsconsulting.com

This book is great for experienced developers whose past experience with JavaScript has left a bad taste in their mouth. Modern JavaScript, when understood through this book, is sure to turn former critics into advocates.

New developers will also benefit from thorough explanations that are in layman's terms—not the overly technical jargon that typically acts as a barrier to entry with many technical books.

➤ **Sara Heins**
International Speaker, Django Girls Kansas City Program Director, and Lead Web Developer, Big 6 Media

This book is ideal for beginners as well as intermediate and beyond.

➤ **Shreerang Patwardhan**
Author of *Mastering jQuery Mobile*, Senior Software Engineer, Macy's Inc.

I would definitely recommend this book to others on my team. I believe that most, if not all, of my team could benefit from reading this book.

➤ **Nick McGinness**
Software Engineer, Direct Supply

Simplifying JavaScript

Writing Modern JavaScript with ES5, ES6, and Beyond

Joe Morgan

The Pragmatic Bookshelf

Raleigh, North Carolina

Many of the designations used by manufacturers and sellers to distinguish their products are claimed as trademarks. Where those designations appear in this book, and The Pragmatic Programmers, LLC was aware of a trademark claim, the designations have been printed in initial capital letters or in all capitals. The Pragmatic Starter Kit, The Pragmatic Programmer, Pragmatic Programming, Pragmatic Bookshelf, PragProg and the linking *g* device are trademarks of The Pragmatic Programmers, LLC.

Every precaution was taken in the preparation of this book. However, the publisher assumes no responsibility for errors or omissions, or for damages that may result from the use of information (including program listings) contained herein.

Our Pragmatic books, screencasts, and audio books can help you and your team create better software and have more fun. Visit us at *https://pragprog.com*.

The team that produced this book includes:

Publisher: Andy Hunt
VP of Operations: Janet Furlow
Managing Editor: Brian MacDonald
Supervising Editor: Jacquelyn Carter
Development Editor: Andrea Stewart
Copy Editor: Nancy Rapoport
Indexing: Potomac Indexing, LLC
Layout: Gilson Graphics

For sales, volume licensing, and support, please contact *support@pragprog.com*.

For international rights, please contact *rights@pragprog.com*.

ISBN-13: 978-1-68050-288-6
Book version: P1.0—April 2018

To Bob and Eric for giving me a foundation

Contents

Introduction

Ever get the feeling you've woken up and everything's different? If you've looked at modern JavaScript, you may feel like you woke up in a new world where nothing's the same.

Yesterday, you were tweaking a simple jQuery accordion. Today, you look at some JavaScript code and the ubiquitous jQuery $ operator is gone. In its place are lots of strange dots (...) and strange symbols (=>) (the spread operator and arrow functions, as you'll soon learn). Sure, some things look familiar, such as class, but even that seems to be unpredictable (where are the private methods?).

Are you perplexed? Maybe a little excited? Well, I have good news for you: Everything has changed for the better.

When the ECMAScript 6 spec was released—ES6 for short—JavaScript code changed dramatically. The changes were so substantial that after reading this book you'll be able to tell at a glance which code was written with pre-ES6 syntax and which code was written with post-ES6 syntax. JavaScript now is different. Modern JavaScript is any code composed with post-ES6 syntax.

Modern JavaScript is a pleasure to write. I'm a long-time unrepentant JavaScript fan, but I'll admit that I found the old syntax a little clunky at times, and it was pretty hard to defend. Modern JavaScript is better. But it's changed significantly, and catching up can be hard.

How To Use This Book

In this book, you'll learn to write modern JavaScript from the ground up. But I'm not going to throw a bunch of syntax at you. I want you to learn to think in terms of contemporary JavaScript. You'll see every piece of syntax with a recommendation for not just *how* to use it, but *when* to use it.

Also, I'm not going to run through every minor syntax change. I know your time is valuable, so I'll only show you syntax that has high impact and that's something you'll use over and over again. You can deal with edge cases when they arise. This book will give you the best features and nothing else.

Throughout the book, you'll see why the syntax changes aren't random—they follow a simple set of principles designed to make the language easier to read and write. Modern JavaScript is simple, predictable, readable, and flexible. And every new piece of syntax should be evaluated in those terms, including syntax that isn't yet part of the spec.

And because modern JavaScript has as many paradigm changes as there are syntax changes, you'll spend some time reviewing older JavaScript concepts to see how you can use them in a modern context. This is important because JavaScript was previously written primarily using libraries (jQuery above all else), and it was easy to plug in just enough code to get something working without understanding the underlying concepts. As more code projects incorporate JavaScript as part of major features, and not just a handful of plugins, you'll need to understand concepts you may have glossed over before.

For example, you might have safely ignored syntax changes in ES5. You could use array methods such as map() and reduce() for several years, but you might have ignored them because browsers weren't fully compatible and because transpilers weren't yet mature. Array methods are now essential parts of good code. It's worth taking a step back to review them.

Still, I know you have plenty to do every day—that's why this book follows a tips format that allows you to jump in and out at will. You don't need to read this straight through. I'll reference syntax from previous and future tips so that you can jump around as you need to. Keep a copy at your desk and skim it during a break, or load it up on your phone so you can get a quick tip in while waiting at the dentist office.

When learning new syntax, the most important thing you can do is read code. And the best code is real code. You won't see foo-bar examples or lots of math expressions in this book. Instead, you'll work with strings, objects, currency, email addresses, and the like. In other words, the code samples you see will be close to life. This adds a little complexity to the examples, but it will ultimately make it much easier for you to internalize the ideas so that you can bring them into your code quickly and easily.

Finally, every sample is available in a repo for this book. The code has nearly 100 percent test coverage, so jump in and try ideas out. To get things working, you'll need at least Node.js version 8.5 installed. You'll also occasionally want to try code in a browser. Be sure to use a modern browser such as Chrome, Edge, or Internet Explorer 11+.

Whom This Book Is For

This book is for anyone who has a little programming experience. It helps to have some JavaScript experience, but that's not strictly necessary. I'll assume that you know some basic programming concepts, such as loops, conditionals, functions, and classes. In short, if you've seen modern JavaScript and you're excited to learn more, then this book is for you.

You may feel like you woke up in a strange new world. That's not a bad thing. In fact, this new world is awesome—the coffee's brewing, and the aroma of fresh-baked danishes makes this new world a place you want to wake up to. JavaScript is better than ever—it's time to enjoy it.

Online Resources

You can also find the code on github[1] or on the book's Pragmatic Bookshelf website.[2] The website also includes a handy community forum if you'd like to reach out for help along the way. Thanks in advance for reporting any issues that you find in the book code or text via the errata form, also conveniently found on the book website.

To stay up-to-date on new syntax changes, you can follow me on twitter— @joesmorgan[3]—or online at thejoemorgan.com.[4]

Acknowledgments

First, thanks to anyone who's ever sent out a tweet, written a blog post, submitted a pull request, spoken at a conference, answered a Stack Overflow question, or done anything to contribute to the greater JavaScript ecosystem. A language is only as good as its community. We have one of the best.

Thank you to my wife, Dyan, and my children, Theo and Bea, for putting up with my crazy schedule. Thanks to my parents, Nathan and Lorraine, for giving me plenty of sticks, string, and duct tape, which led me to my lifelong love of building and exploring. And a big thanks to Martha Vogel for all the extra help so I could carve out a few precious hours to write.

Thank you to the staff of the University of Wisconsin Center for Limnology, the librarians of the University of Wisconsin, the staff of MERIT library, the

---

1. https://github.com/jsmapr1/simplifying-js
2. https://pragprog.com/book/es6tips/simplifying-javascript
3. https://twitter.com/joesmorgan
4. http://thejoemorgan.com

librarians and staff of the Johnson County Library, the engineers at Red Nova Labs, the web team and marketing department at the University of Kansas, the engineers at Builder Designs, the staff at DEG, and anyone else who has taught me a thing or two about programming and communicating ideas.

Thank you to Sara Heins, Ashley Sullins, Adam Braun, and Katie McCurry for help with marketing.

Thank you to the good people at Pragmatic Programmers for the opportunity to write about JavaScript. Thank you to Brian MacDonald for helping me get started. And a big thank you to my editor, Andrea Stewart, for helping me find my voice and keeping the process smooth.

Finally, thank you to all my technical reviewers: Craig Hess, Frank Ruiz, Jessica Janiuk, Mark Poko, Nick McGinness, Ryan Heap, Shreerang Patwardhan, Stefan Turalski, and Vasile Boris. You kept me honest and made the book even better.

Joe Morgan
Lawrence, KS, April 2018

CHAPTER 1

Signal Intention with Variable Assignment

Before we begin, I have a question for you. How many variables did you declare in your code yesterday? It doesn't matter what language you were writing. Was it ten? A hundred? How about over the last week? Last month? Probably a lot.

Now think about how many variables you read yesterday. Maybe you read your own code, or maybe you were skimming someone else's. Did you see a hundred variables? a thousand? Chances are, you don't have a clue.

Now if I asked you how many curried functions you saw yesterday, I bet you'd know the answer. I can tell you that I saw exactly one curried function yesterday. I know that because even though there's been lots of ink spilled about curried functions in JavaScript (and I'll be spilling some myself in Tip 34, *Maintain Single Responsibility Parameters with Partially Applied Functions*, on page 160), it's not nearly as common as a simple variable declaration. In fact, if you've never heard of a curried function, that's even more proof that they aren't nearly as important as simple variable declaration. We spend so much time thinking and teaching complex concepts, but something as simple as variable declaration will affect your life and the lives of other developers in a much more significant way.

You're about to rethink JavaScript code from the ground up. And that means you need to start at the most basic level: assigning information to variables. So that's the theme for our first chapter.

Modern JavaScript has several new ways to declare variables. Whenever you start to write a variable, you just need to ask yourself if this will make the code more readable and predictable for the next developer. You'll find that it actually changes how you write quite a bit.

You're going to look at two new variable declaration types. The first, const, doesn't allow you to reassign the variable (which you'll see is a good thing).

The second, let, will allow reassignment, but it's block scoped and will protect you from potential scope conflicts. Finally, you'll learn how to use template literals to create new strings from your variables.

The tips in this chapter will help you understand how your decisions will affect the rest of the code, and also how your decisions will affect anyone else who might eventually pick up and read your code.

I hope that as you read this chapter, you begin to critically examine the JavaScript that you write every day. The bonus is that with just a handful of tips, you'll be well on your way to writing JavaScript code that's more simple and expressive. And don't be surprised if the mindset you learn when assessing variable declarations flows out into the rest of your code. After all, it's the most common decision you'll make while you write—a decision you'll make 10, 20, 100 times tomorrow, and next week, and next month.

Ready? Good. Let's begin.

Tip 1

Signal Unchanging Values with const

In this tip, you'll learn to use const to avoid reassignment and signal your intention to other developers.

Modern JavaScript introduced several new variable declarations, which is great. But it also introduced a new problem: Which variable declaration should be the default? And when should we use another type?

In the past, you had only one option for non-global variable assignment: var. Now there are many different options—var, let, and const—and each one has an appropriate usage. Try and keep things simple. In most cases, const is the best choice, not because it allows you to do the most, but because it lets you do the least. It has restrictions that make your code more readable.

ECMAScript 6

ECMAScript is the official technical specification for JavaScript. JavaScript incorporated major syntax changes in ECMAScript 5 and ECMAScript 6, which are referred to as ES5 and ES6. Going forward, the spec will be updated yearly. Most developers now refer to the spec by year, such as ES2017.

const is a variable declaration that you can't reassign within the context of the block. In other words, once you establish it, it can't be changed. That doesn't mean it's immutable—a value that cannot be changed. If it's assigned to an array, the items in the array can be changed. We'll look at this more shortly.

It may seem odd to developers in other languages with a constant assignment that const is the preferred declaration. In those languages, a constant is usually something you'd write in ALLCAPS and only use on rare occasions to denote things that are never going to change, like the first digits of pi.

In JavaScript, though, const is a great default choice precisely because it can't be reassigned. When you assign a value, you aren't just declaring a piece of information. You're also signaling what you plan to do with that information. When you assign values and signal that they won't be changed, you give future developers (including yourself!) the knowledge that they can forget about a value while they skim the code. And when you're reading a large amount of code that you haven't seen before, you'll be happy that you can forget some of what you read.

Let's assume you're fixing a bug in a piece of code. You're skimming through the code to get an idea of how it works and to see if you can guess where the problem might be. Consider two programs. The first program uses const to assign a variable while the second uses var to assign a variable.

variables/const/const.js
```
const taxRate = 0.1;

const total = 100 + (100 * taxRate);

// Skip 100 lines of code

return `Your Order is ${total}`;
```

variables/const/const.js
```
var taxRate = 0.1;

var total = 100 + (100 * taxRate);

// Skip 100 lines of code

return `Your Order is ${total}`;
```

They look nearly identical, but the first is much easier to understand. Ignore the fact that a block of code shouldn't be 100 lines long; you have a large amount of code where lots of changes are occurring.

With the first block, you know exactly what will get returned: Your Order is 110. You know this because total is a constant that can't be reassigned. With the second block, you have no idea what the return value is going to be. You are going to need to go through the 100 lines of additional code looking for loops or conditionals or reassignments or anything that might change the value. Maybe the code is adding a shipping cost. Maybe additional items will be added to the total. Maybe a discount is going to be applied and the total will drop.

You have no idea what the total is going to be when it's assigned with var. When you assign a variable with const, it removes one additional piece of information that you need to retain in your head while reading code. Consider one last example:

variables/const/const.js
```
const taxRate = 0.1;
const shipping = 5.00;

let total = 100 + (100 * taxRate) + shipping;

// Skip 100 lines of code

return `Your Order is ${total}`;
```

Take a moment and think about what you can be certain of from this code. You know you *can't* be sure of the total. The developers have signaled that taxRate and shipping are unchanging (if only that were true), but the total isn't permanent. You know this value can't be trusted.

The best case is to know that an assignment won't change. The second best case is to know that it *might* change. If you can see that the developers used const regularly and let rarely, you can guess areas of change.

Make all variable assignments either a known-known or a known-unknown.

There's one important consideration when using const: A value assigned to const *is not immutable*. In other words, you can't reassign the variable, but you *can* change the value. That may seem contradictory, but here it is in practice.

variables/const/const.js
```
const discountable = [];

// Skip some lines

for (let i = 0; i < cart.length; i++) {
  if (cart[i].discountAvailable) {
    discountable.push(cart[i]);
  }
}
```

This is perfectly valid code. Even though discountable is assigned with const, you can still push items to it. This creates the exact problem we saw earlier: You can't be certain of what you'll see later in the code. For objects, arrays, or other collections, you'll need to be more disciplined.

There's no clear consensus on what you should use, but your best bet is to avoid mutations as much as possible.

Here's an example of the previous code written without mutations.

variables/const/const.js
```
const discountable = cart.filter(item => item.discountAvailable);
```

Same result. No mutations. If the code is confusing, you can jump to Chapter 5, *Simplify Loops*, on page 87 for more information about array methods.

For now, just use const as a default. Once the code changes to the point where const is no longer appropriate, you can try a different declaration.

In the next tip, you'll see precisely when const is no longer an appropriate choice and why you should use a new declaration: let.

Tip 2

Reduce Scope Conflicts with let and const

In this tip, you'll learn that in cases where a value is going to change, let is the best choice.

You saw in the previous tip that when you're working with variables, you're better off avoiding reassignment. But what do you do in situations where you really need to reassign a variable? In those cases, you should use let.

let is similar to var because it can be reassigned, but unlike var, which is lexically scoped, let is block scoped. You'll explore scope more in Tip 3, *Isolate Information with Block Scoped Variables*, on page 10. For now, just know that block scoped variables exist only in blocks, such as an if block or a for loop. Outside those blocks, they aren't accessible. As a rule, this means the variable doesn't exist outside the curly braces in which it was declared.

To see how a block scoped or a lexically scoped variable can change code, consider an example. This code looks for the lowest price for an item. To find the lowest price, it makes three simple checks:

- If there is no inventory: Return 0.
- If there is a sale price and sale inventory: Return sale price.
- If there is no sale price or no sale inventory: Return price.

variables/let/problem.js

```
Line 1  function getLowestPrice(item) {
          var count = item.inventory;
          var price = item.price;

     5    if (item.salePrice) {
            var count = item.saleInventory;
            if (count > 0) {
              price = item.salePrice;
            }
    10    }

          if (count) {
            return price;
          }
    15
          return 0;
        }
```

Take a moment and see if you can find the bug.

Look at each expected outcome and see what you can find. Alternatively, you can run the test suite.[1]

Did you find it? The problem is that you're reassigning a variable to the same variable name.

If you have an item with no inventory and no sale price, the item.salePrice conditional will be skipped and you'll get 0.

```
variables/let/let.spec.js
const item = {
  inventory: 0,
  price: 3,
  salePrice: 0,
  saleInventory: 0,
};
```

Next, if you have a sale price and a sale inventory, you get the sale price. In this case, the returned value will be 2.

```
variables/let/let.spec.js
const item = {
  inventory: 3,
  price: 3,
  salePrice: 2,
  saleInventory: 1,
};
```

Finally, if you have a sale price but no sale inventory, you expect to get the regular price, 3. What you actually get is 0.

```
variables/let/let.spec.js
const item = {
  inventory: 3,
  price: 3,
  salePrice: 2,
  saleInventory: 0,
};
```

If you're still a little confused, that's okay. It's a tricky bug. The problem is that you declare the variable count on lines 2 to 3. There's a sale price, so you go into the next if block. At this point, you redeclare the variable count on line 6. Now the problem is that this is set to 0 because there's no more sale inventory. By the time you get to the next if block on line 12, the inventory is wrong. It looks like there's no sale inventory and no regular priced inventory.

---

1. https://pragprog.com/titles/es6tips/source_code

Even though you have a regular inventory, you're accidentally checking the sale inventory and returning the wrong value.

You might want to dismiss this problem as trivial. But bugs like this are subtle and hard to catch if they make it into production.

Fortunately, you can avoid this issue using let. In fact, let helps you avoid this issue in two ways.

let is block scoped, which again means any variable declared inside a block doesn't exist outside the block.

variables/let/let.js
```javascript
function getLowestPrice(item) {
  let count = item.inventory;
  let price = item.price;

  if (item.salePrice) {
    let count = item.saleInventory;
    if (count > 0) {
      price = item.salePrice;
    }
  }

  if (count) {
    return price;
  }

  return 0;
}
```

In this case, using let to declare the count variable in the if block isn't going to conflict with the count variable declared at the start of the function.

Of course, let isn't the only variable declaration that's block scoped. const is also block scoped. Because you're never reassigning count, you can use const instead and keep things even more clear, although you'll need to continue to use let to declare price because that may update. Honestly, you should just use different names to keep things clear. The final code would be this:

variables/let/const.js
```javascript
function getLowestPrice(item) {
  const count = item.inventory;
  let price = item.price;

  if (item.salePrice) {
    const saleCount = item.saleInventory;
    if (saleCount > 0) {
      price = item.salePrice;
    }
  }
}
```

```
  if (count) {
    return price;
  }

  return 0;
}
```

As an added bonus, let and const have another protection. You can't redeclare a variable of the same name. With var, you can redeclare a variable of the same name in the same scope. In other words, you can say var price = 1 at, say line 10 and var price = 5 at line 25 with no conflict. This can be a huge problem if you unintentionally reuse a variable name. With let, you can't make this mistake.

This code would generate a TypeError.

variables/let/declaration.js
```
function getLowestPriceDeclaration(item) {
  const count = item.inventory;
  let price = item.price;

  if (!count) {
    return 0;
  }

  // ...

  let price = item.saleInventory ? item.salePrice : item.wholesalePrice;

  return price;
}
```

This issue won't come up often, but it's a nice way to catch a potential bug early in the process.

In the next tip, you'll take a deeper look into scope and how let solves one of the most common and perplexing scope conflicts in JavaScript.

Tip 3

Isolate Information with Block Scoped Variables

In this tip, you'll learn how let *prevents scope conflict in* for *loops and other iterations.*

At one point or another, every developer will make the mistake of capturing the wrong variable during a for loop. The traditional solution involves some pretty advanced JavaScript concepts. Fortunately, the let variable declaration makes this complex issue disappear.

Remember, when you use a block scoped variable declaration, you're creating a variable that's only accessible in the block. A variable declared in an if block isn't available outside the curly braces. A variable declared inside a for loop isn't available outside the curly braces of the for loop. But that doesn't mean you can't access variables declared outside a function. If you declare a block scope variable at the top of a function, it *is* accessible inside the block.

If you declare a lexically scoped variable, however, it's accessible anywhere inside a function. A variable created inside an if block can be accessed anywhere else in the function. In fact, you can even access a variable before it was declared because of a compile process called hoisting.[2]

If that all seems too abstract, that's fine. It's easier to understand in practice. Chances are, if you've encountered a lexical scope issue before, it probably occurred when you were adding a click function to a series of DOM elements:

variables/scope/scope.html
```html
<!doctype html>

<html lang="en">
    <body>
        <ul style="cursor:pointer">
            <li> Say Zero </li>
            <li> Say One </li>
            <li> Say Two </li>
        </ul>
    </body>
    <script>
        const items = document.querySelectorAll('li');
        for(var i = 0; i< items.length; i++) {
            items[i].addEventListener('click', () => {
```

---

2.   https://developer.mozilla.org/en-US/docs/Glossary/Hoisting

```
                alert(i);
            })
        };
    </script>
</html>
```

Open this code in a browser and try clicking on one of the list elements. You'll find that every click will give the same result: 3.

It's tempting to think this is a browser bug, but it's actually more related to how JavaScript assigns variables. It can happen anywhere, even in regular JavaScript code. Let's look at how this issue can occur even in plain JavaScript without DOM manipulation.

If you paste this code into a browser console or a REPL, you'll see the same problem.

variables/scope/problem.js
```
Line 1  function addClick(items) {
     2    for (var i = 0; i < items.length; i++) {
     3      items[i].onClick = function () { return i; };
     4    }
     5    return items;
     6  }
     7  const example = [{}, {}];
     8  const clickSet = addClick(example);
     9  clickSet[0].onClick();
```

Using REPLs

REPL is an acronym for "read evaluate print loop." It is one of the most valuable tools you can have when working with code. A REPL is simply a command-line interface where you type in some code and the REPL immediately evaluates it and returns the result.

For example, type in 2+2 and you'll get 4. These are great when you can't quite remember syntax and want to give it a quick check. I can never remember the method for making a string uppercase, which is a problem when I need to yell something. To refresh my memory, I'll go into a REPL and type 'hi!'.upperCase(), which gives me an error. Then I'll try again with 'hi!'.toUpperCase(); //HI!, which works and off I go.

Where are these REPLs? If you have Node.js installed on your computer (which you should), go to a command line and type node and you'll be dropped into a REPL.

If you are debugging code in a browser, you also have a REPL at your fingertips, though it is called console in most browsers. All modern browsers have developer tools that contain a console of some sort. This is another place where you can type Java-Script code and see immediate results. As a bonus, this will help you check which features are natively implemented on that particular browser.

No matter which array element you try, you'll get the same result.

Why is this happening?

The problem again is scope. Variables assigned with var are functionally scoped (which, again, is technically referred to as lexically scoped). That means that they'll always refer to the last value they're assigned within a function.

When you set a new function on line 3 in the preceding example, you're saying to return the value i whatever it may be at the time you call the code. You are *not* saying: return the value of i at the time it's set. As a result, because i belongs to the function, the value changes on each loop iteration.

The traditional solution is complicated, and it can confuse even the most experienced JavaScript developers.

variables/scope/curry.js
```
function addClick(items) {
  for (var i = 0; i < items.length; i++) {
    items[i].onClick = (function (i) {
      return function () {
        return i;
      };
    }(i));
  }
  return items;
}
const example = [{}, {}];
const clickSet = addClick(example);
clickSet[0].onClick();
```

It involves a combination of closures (creating a variable inside a function for another function to use), higher-order functions (functions that return other functions), and self-invoking functions. If you don't understand that, it's fine. You'll learn more about higher-order functions in Tip 34, *Maintain Single Responsibility Parameters with Partially Applied Functions*, on page 160.

Fortunately, you don't need to understand these higher concepts quite yet. If you rewrite the preceding code using let, you'll get the same results without the extra code clutter. Test out the following code in a browser console or REPL and you'll get the results you were expecting.

variables/scope/scope.js
```
Line 1 function addClick(items) {
   2   for (let i = 0; i < items.length; i++) {
   3     items[i].onClick = function () { return i; };
   4   }
   5   return items;
   6 }
```

```
7  const example = [{}, {}];
8  const clickSet = addClick(example);
9  clickSet[0].onClick();
```

Looking at line 3, you'll notice the only thing you changed is using let instead of var. Because let is blocked scoped, any variable declared inside the for block belongs *only* to that block. So even if the value changes in another iteration, the value won't change on the previously declared function.

In simpler terms, let locks the value during each iteration of the for loop.

Because let can do nearly everything var can do, it's always best to use let whenever you might otherwise use var.

I hope this gave you some ideas for how to declare variables. You will find in upcoming tips that variable declaration is so important that you may want to restructure whole code blocks to keep declarations clear and predictable.

In the next tip, you'll look at how to transform data to readable strings using template literals.

Tip 4

Convert Variables to Readable Strings with Template Literals

In this tip, you will learn how to convert variables into new strings without concatenation.

Strings are messy. That's all there is to it. When you're pulling information from strings, you have to deal with the ugliness of natural language: capitalization, punctuation, misspellings. It's a headache.

Collecting information into strings is less painful, but it can still get ugly quickly. Combining strings in JavaScript can be particularly rough, especially when you combine strings assigned to variables with strings surrounded by quotes.

Here's a situation that comes up all the time: You need to build a URL. In this case, you're building a link to an image on a cloud service. Your cloud service is pretty great, though. In addition to hosting the asset, you can pass query parameters that will convert the asset in a variety of ways (height, width, and so on).

To keep things relatively simple, you're going to make a function that creates a URL by combining your cloud provider URL with the ID of the image and the width as a query parameter.

To keep things complicated, you're going to combine regular strings with strings that are returned from a function, strings that are assigned to variables, and strings that are converted right before concatenation. You're going to use a function (implemented elsewhere) that will return a cloud provider such as pragprog.com/cloud. Your function will take ID and width as parameters, but it will need to parse the width to make sure it's an integer.

URLs get particularly ugly because you have to add slashes between the parts of a route along with the building blocks of queries such as ?, =, and &. Traditionally, you have to combine each piece with a + sign.

The final result looks like this:

variables/literals/problem.js
```
function generateLink(image, width) {
  const widthInt = parseInt(width, 10);
  return 'https://' + getProvider() + '/' + image + '?width=' + widthInt;
}
```

There's a lot going on there, and the combination of information and + signs doesn't help. And this is a particularly simple URL. They can get more complicated fast. What if the route was longer or you needed an additional four parameters? These things get long.

Fortunately, you can cut down the complexity quite a bit using template literals. Template literals are a simple syntax that lets you combine strings along with JavaScript expressions to create a new string.

There are only two things you need to know: First, a template literal is surrounded by backticks (`) instead of single or double quotes. Second, anything that's not a string (including strings assigned to variables) needs to be surrounded by a special designator: a $ sign with the variables or other JavaScript code in curly braces: `${stuff}`.

You'll most often use this for combining strings and variables.

```
variables/literals/literals.js
function greet(name) {
  return `Hi, ${name}`;
}
greet('Leo');
'Hi, Leo';
```

But you can also perform JavaScript actions. For example, you can call a method on a object. In this case, you're converting a string to uppercase:

```
variables/literals/literals.js
function yell(name) {
  return `HI, ${name.toUpperCase()}!`;
}
greet('Pankaj');
'HI, PANKAJ!';
```

You can even perform more complex computations, such as combining math calculations. Really, you can perform any action in the curly braces, but it would only make sense to perform actions that return a string or integer.

```
variables/literals/literals.js
function leapYearConverter(age) {
  return `You'd be ${Math.floor(age / 4)} if born on a leap year.`;
}
leapYearConverter(34);
// "You'd be 8 if born on a leap year."
```

Try not to do much with the curly braces. It can be more cluttered than it's worth. If you need to do heavy data conversions, perform the action outside the template literal and assign the result to a variable.

You now have all the tools to rewrite your original string concatenation as a single template literal. Take a moment and try it out.

Your solution probably looks something like this:

```
variables/literals/literals.js
function generateLink(image, width) {
  return `https://${getProvider()}/${image}?width=${parseInt(width, 10)}`;
}
```

Doesn't that look significantly cleaner? Template literals are such an improvement on string concatenation that you should rarely ever combine strings with traditional concatenation. The only time it would be better is if you're combining two variables with no additional information. Even in that case, you may still use template literals because those backticks are a clue to other developers that you're returning a string.

In the next chapter, you're going to learn about how to use collections of data. You'll be building on many of the ideas in this chapter as you make choices between new and existing collections.

CHAPTER 2

Manage Data Collections with Arrays

The ancient Greek poet Archilochus wrote, "A fox knows many things, but a hedgehog one important thing." The great historian Isaiah Berlin said all thinkers are either hedgehogs or foxes. I think the same is true of syntax.

As you've seen, const is a hedgehog. It can only do one thing—make an unchanging declaration. By only doing one thing, it makes your code readable and predictable. As you'll see in upcoming tips, array methods are all hedgehogs. They can do only one thing on an array. But they do it well, so you can safely predict outcomes without diving into the details.

For the most part, you want to stick with syntax that does one thing very well. But there are times when you need things to be flexible. An array is the ultimate fox because it can do many things. In fact, it can do almost anything you'd ever want for a collection of information. More importantly, many other collections use concepts that you'd most often associate with arrays.

For example, when you have a string, 'hedgehog', you have a lot of available actions you'd normally perform on arrays. You can get the size: 'hedgehog'.length will return 8. You can also pick out individual letters by index: 'hedgehog'[3] will return 'g'. There are so many other methods that it would take too long to list them all.

These methods don't belong to arrays specifically (they rely on a property called Iterator), but they're most intuitively connected to arrays. When you study arrays carefully, you'll gain many insights into other data structures. Arrays know many things. They are foxes.

In this chapter, you'll see that arrays are becoming better than ever. Not only are they a good choice for many data needs, but they have new syntax that reduces many common actions to one-liners while simultaneously reducing mutations that can cause subtle bugs. And pay attention—you'll see the same ideas in later tips.

To begin, you'll see how data can always be converted to arrays, including converting other collections (such as objects) to arrays when necessary. From there, you'll learn new syntax, such as includes(), to test existence in arrays and, crucially, the spread operator symbolized by three dots (...). The spread operator is so important in the modern use of arrays that the next two tips will explore how the spread operator changes how you use arrays in your code. Pay close attention—you'll see the spread operator in many future tips.

To keep code readable, you should stick with simple, predictable approaches (hedgehogs). But to make code flexible, you need arrays to move between structures. It's a tough balancing act, but you need both. Everything you do in JavaScript will be easier if you have a clear understanding of arrays.

Time to jump in and see how arrays provide a level of flexibility you won't find in most collections.

Tip 5

Create Flexible Collections with Arrays

In this tip, you'll learn how arrays maximize flexibility and give you a foundation for understanding all other collections.

In JavaScript, there used to be only two structures for collections of data: arrays and objects. That list is growing. Now there are maps, sets, weakmaps, weaksets, objects, and arrays.

When choosing a collection, you have to ask yourself what you need to do with the information. If you need to manipulate it in any way (add, remove, sort, filter, alter all members), then arrays are often the best collection. And even when you don't use an array, you'll almost certainly use ideas that you'd associate with arrays.

Arrays have a remarkable amount of flexibility. Because arrays preserve order, you can add and remove items according to their position or determine if they have a position at all. You can sort to give the array a new order as you'll see in Tip 9, *Avoid Sort Confusion with the Spread Operator*, on page 34.

```
arrays/arrays/arrays.js
const team = [
  'Joe',
  'Dyan',
  'Bea',
  'Theo',
];
function alphabetizeTeam(team) {
  return [...team].sort();
  // ['Bea', 'Dyan', 'Joe', 'Theo']
}
```

Interestingly, order is not technically guaranteed,[1] but it's safe to assume that it will work in nearly all circumstances.

With array methods such as map(), filter(), and reduce(), you can alter or update the information easily with single lines, as you'll see starting with Tip 22, *Create Arrays of a Similar Size with map()*, on page 98.

---

1. https://stackoverflow.com/questions/34955787/is-a-javascript-array-order-guaranteed

arrays/arrays/arrays.js

```
const staff = [
  {
    name: 'Wesley',
    position: 'musician',
  },
  {
    name: 'Davis',
    position: 'engineer',
  },
];

function getMusicians(staff) {
  return staff.filter(member => member.position === 'musician');
  // [{name: 'Wesley', position: 'musician'}]
}
```

You may notice some strange looking syntax. Don't worry—you'll get to it soon. A lot of the new syntax in ES5 and ES6 is related to arrays. That should be a clue that they're valued highly in the JavaScript community.

Still, you'll need to use other collections. Yet, a solid understanding of arrays will greatly improve your code because arrays are at the heart of many popular data manipulations. For example, if you need to iterate over an object, the first thing you'd do is get the keys into an array with Object.keys() and then iterate over those. You're using an array as a bridge between the object and a loop.

arrays/arrays/arrays.js

```
const game1 = {
  player: 'Jim Jonas',
  hits: 2,
  runs: 1,
  errors: 0,
};

const game2 = {
  player: 'Jim Jonas',
  hits: 3,
  runs: 0,
  errors: 1,
};

const total = {};

const stats = Object.keys(game1);
for (let i = 0; i < stats.length; i++) {
  const stat = stats[i];
  if (stat !== 'player') {
    total[stat] = game1[stat] + game2[stat];
  }
}
```

```
// {
//   hits: 5,
//   runs: 1,
//   errors: 1
// }
```

Arrays seem to pop up everywhere because they have a built-in iterable.[2] An iterable is merely a way for the code to go through a collection one item at a time while knowing its current position. Any action you can perform on an array you can also perform on any data type that has an iterable (such as strings) or one that you can quickly transform into an iterable (as with Object.keys()).

If you know that you can create a new array with the spread operator, as you'll see in Tip 7, *Mold Arrays with the Spread Operator*, on page 25, then you know that you can create a new Map with the spread operator because it also has a built-in iterable, as you'll see in Tip 14, *Iterate Over Key-Value Data with Map and the Spread Operator*, on page 60.

Finally, you can express nearly every collection concept in the form of an array, which means you can easily convert from an array to a specialized collection and back again. Think about an object as a key-value store.

arrays/arrays/arrays.js
```
const dog = {
  name: 'Don',
  color: 'black',
};

dog.name;
// Don
```

You can describe that same concept, a key-value store, as an array of arrays. The internal arrays contain only two items. The first item is a key. The second item is the value. This particular structure, an array consisting of two items, is also called a pair. Finding the value for a specific key is merely a matter of finding the pair with the correct key name and then returning the second item.

arrays/arrays/arrays.js
```
const dogPair = [
  ['name', 'Don'],
  ['color', 'black'],
];
```

---

2. https://developer.mozilla.org/en-US/docs/Web/JavaScript/Guide/Iterators_and_Generators#Built-in_iterables

```
function getName(dog) {
  return dog.find(attribute => {
    return attribute[0] === 'name';
  })[1];
}
```

Admittedly, that's a lot of extra code for something so simple. You certainly wouldn't put this in a code base, but it's good to know that an object *could* be an array of pairs.

In fact, you'll use pairs to convert data between the Map object and an array. And now that the TC39 committee has finalized the spec to convert an object to an array of pairs using Object.entries(),[3] you'll be able to use any array technique on objects with a quick conversion.

The TC39 Committee

What does it mean that something is part of a finalized spec? The JavaScript spec is determined by a committee called the TC39 committee. They take proposals for syntax changes through a standard process before defining their official specifications (or spec). You'll often hear developers refer to "stage 1" or "stage 2" features when talking about features still in the review process. This just means that they are still being finalized but are on the way to adoption as part of the spec. After a piece of syntax is approved, browsers start to work on native implementations.

In other words, there are always new syntax changes on the way. Up until ES6, you would refer to syntax changes by version such as ES5 or ES6. From now on, you will see syntax changes by year such as ES2017, ES2018, and so on. To add to the confusion, because most JavaScript will still need to be compiled to earlier syntax to be compatible with older browsers, you can use syntax before it's final. This can be dangerous, but occasionally there are features that are so popular they are affectively adopted by the community before they are officially approved. New syntax features such as async and await or the Object spread are used before they are official.

Having a deep understanding of arrays, and most iterables by proxy, will let you grasp not only many of the new ES6 features that we're about to explore, but also many new features that are coming soon.

In the next tip, you'll begin to work with arrays by learning how testing existence in arrays has become even easier with includes().

---

3.   https://github.com/tc39/proposal-object-values-entries

| Tip 6 |

Check Existence in an Array with Includes()

In this tip, you'll learn how to find out if a value exists in an array without checking position.

It's easy to get so caught up in the big exciting changes in a language (such as the spread operator, which you'll see in a moment) that you miss the small changes that simplify common tasks.

Arrays now have an easy improvement to handle a common problem: testing existence. Testing existence is an important action, and it's crucial in everything from ternaries (Tip 18, *Check Data Quickly with the Ternary Operator*, on page 79), to short circuiting (Tip 19, *Maximize Efficiency with Short Circuiting*, on page 82), to most conditionals in general.

Testing existence with JavaScript arrays has always been a little clunky. For example, if you want to see if an array contains a certain string, you check to see if the string has a position (position being another feature of an iterable). If the position exists, you'll get the index. If not, you get -1. The problem is that the index can be 0, which evaluates to false (also known as being falsy). This means the existence can be true, but the check can evaluate to false.

```
arrays/includes/problem.js
const sections = ['shipping'];

function displayShipping(sections) {
  if (sections.indexOf('shipping')) {
    return true;
  }
  return false;
}
// false
```

Because of this unfortunate situation, a position at 0 being falsy, you have to compare the index against a number and not just test that it's truthy. It's not a big problem, but it's just extra code to remember. Jump ahead to Tip 17, *Shorten Conditionals with Falsy Values*, on page 75 for more on falsy values.

arrays/includes/greater.js
```
const sections = ['contact', 'shipping'];

function displayShipping(sections) {
  return sections.indexOf('shipping') > -1;
}

// true
```

Fortunately, another feature coming up in ES2017 will eliminate that boiler-plate comparison. The new array method, called includes(),[4] will check to see if a value exists in an array and return a Boolean of true or false.

You can rewrite the preceding code with a simple check.

arrays/includes/includes.js
```
const sections = ['contact', 'shipping'];

function displayShipping(sections) {
  return sections.includes('shipping');
}
```

This may seem like a trivial change, but after writing -1 over and over in a codebase, or even worse, forgetting and getting false negatives on a zero-indexed value, it's a welcome change.

Now that you've seen how integral arrays are to JavaScript, you'll dive into them a little more as we explore some of the new features that make them even more exciting and powerful. It's best to get comfortable with arrays because they're everywhere in JavaScript. And even if you aren't using them directly, don't be surprised if a lot of what you learn about arrays begins to show up in other collections.

In the next tip, you'll learn how to use the most interesting and powerful new technique for working with arrays: the spread operator.

---

4.   https://github.com/tc39/Array.prototype.includes/

| Tip 7 |

Mold Arrays with the Spread Operator

In this tip, you'll learn how to simplify many array actions with the spread operator.

As you've seen, arrays provide an incredible amount of flexibility for working with data. But the number of methods that an array contains can be confusing, and it could lead you to some problems with mutations and side effects. Fortunately, the spread operator gives you a way to create and manipulate arrays quickly with minimal code.

The spread operator, symbolized with three dots (...), may be the most widely used new feature in JavaScript. You're likely to find it in nearly every file containing ES6+ syntax.

That said, it's hard to take the spread operator seriously. I certainly didn't. What it does is so mundane: It converts an array to a list of items. Turns out, that tiny action has many benefits that we'll explore in the next few tips.

The benefits don't end with just arrays. You'll see the spread operator over and over. It pops up in the Map collection, as you'll see in Tip 14, *Iterate Over Key-Value Data with Map and the Spread Operator*, on page 60. You'll use a variation called the rest operator in functions, as you'll see in Tip 31, *Pass a Variable Number of Arguments with the Rest Operator*, on page 143. And you can use the spread operator on any data structure or class property using generators, as you'll see in Tip 41, *Create Iterable Properties with Generators*, on page 192.

I hope that I've sparked your interest. To start, try using the spread operator on a simple array.

You begin with an array of items.

```
const cart = ['Naming and Necessity', 'Alice in Wonderland'];
```

You then use the spread operator (...) to turn that into a list—a series of items that you can use in parameters or to build an array:

```
const cart = ['Naming and Necessity', 'Alice in Wonderland'];
...cart
```

If you try this out in a REPL or a browser console, you'll get an error. The syntax is correct, but you can't use the spread operator on its own. You can't, for example, assign the output to a variable. You have to spread the information into something.

```
const copyCart = [...cart];
// ['Naming and Necessity', 'Alice in Wonderland']
```

Now, before you think "big deal" and skip to the next tip, I want you to know I understand. I didn't appreciate the spread operator until I started seeing it pop up everywhere. And I didn't love it until I started using it. But now it's my favorite ES6 feature by far.

To see how powerful the spread operator can be, start with a simple task: removing an item from an array. Here's an approach using only a loop:

arrays/spread/problem.js
```
function removeItem(items, removable) {
  const updated = [];
  for (let i = 0; i < items.length; i++) {
    if (items[i] !== removable) {
      updated.push(items[i]);
    }
  }
  return updated;
}
```

This isn't bad code. But there's certainly a lot of it. It's a good rule to keep things as simple as you can. The more clutter and loops that exist, the harder it will be to read and understand the code.

In trying to simplify, you may stumble on an array method called splice(). It removes an item from an array, and that's exactly what you want! If you refactor the preceding function, it does become more simple.

arrays/spread/splice.js
```
function removeItem(items, removable) {
  const index = items.indexOf(removable);
  items.splice(index, 1);
  return items;
}
```

The problem with splice() is that is mutates the original array. Take a look at the following example and see if you can spot the problem:

arrays/spread/splice.js
```
const books = ['practical vim', 'moby dick', 'the dark tower'];
const recent = removeItem(books, 'moby dick');
const novels = removeItem(books, 'practical vim');
```

What do you think the novels array will contain?

The only book it will contain is 'the dark tower'. When you called removeItem() the first time, you passed it books and got back the array without 'moby dick'. But it also changed the books array. When you passed it to the next function, it was only two items long.

This is why mutations can be so hazardous, particularly if you're using them in a function. You may not expect the information passed to be fundamentally different. Notice in this case that you're even assigning books with const. You may assume this won't be mutated, but that isn't always the case.

Splice may seem like a good alternative to a for loop, but mutations can create so much confusion that you're better off avoiding them whenever possible.

Finally, there's one last option. Arrays also have a method called slice(), which returns a part of an array without changing the original array. When you're using slice, you pass a startpoint and endpoint, and you get everything in between. Alternatively, you can pass just a startpoint and get everything from that point until the end of the array. Then you can use concat() to put the pieces of the array back together.

```
arrays/spread/slice.js
function removeItem(items, removable) {
  const index = items.indexOf(removable);
  return items.slice(0, index).concat(items.slice(index + 1));
}
```

This code is pretty great. You get the new array back without changing the original array, and you avoid a lot of code. However, it isn't clear what's being returned. Another developer would need to know that concat() joins two arrays into a single flat array. There's no visual clue for what you're doing.

This is where the spread operator comes in. Combined with a slice, the spread operator turns both sub-arrays into a list that's placed back into square brackets. It actually looks like an array. And more importantly, it gives you a smaller array without affecting the larger array.

```
arrays/spread/spread.js
function removeItem(items, removable) {
  const index = items.indexOf(removable);
  return [...items.slice(0, index), ...items.slice(index + 1)];
}
```

Notice a few things about this code. There are no mutations. It's easy to read. It's simple. It's reusable. It's predictable. In short, it has all of your favorite attributes.

You can actually further improve this code. As you'll see in Tip 23, *Pull Out Subsets of Data with filter() and find()*, on page 102, you can pass a function that removes a specific item in an array. There are many ways to perform the same action. Go for the one that best communicates your intentions.

This is just the beginning. The spread operator lets you quickly pull out the items of an array with very few characters. And you'll always put them back into a structure that you can quickly and easily recognize.

If you look back through the four examples, you see that they all work. But the spread is the most readable and the easiest to predict.

The other popular way to use the spread operator is to create a list of arguments for a function. Create a small function to format an array of information.

arrays/spread/spread.js
```
const book = ['Reasons and Persons', 'Derek Parfit', 19.99];

function formatBook(title, author, price) {
  return `${title} by ${author} $${price}`;
}
```

How can you put the information into the function? Try it out. You probably came up with something like this:

arrays/spread/spread.js
```
formatBook(book[0], book[1], book[2]);
```

But there's an even simpler version that you won't have to change if the amount of data on the book changes. For example, say you add a publication year.

If you came up with something like this, great work. Parameters are lists of arguments, so the spread operator allows you to convert an array to a list of parameters quickly and easily.

arrays/spread/spread.js
```
formatBook(...book);
```

Here's the interesting thing: This isn't the only way you can quickly extract information from an array in parameters. You could also pull it out directly using array destructuring. You'll explore destructuring in greater detail in Tip 29, *Access Object Properties with Destructuring*, on page 133.

And that's not all! The spread operator really starts to shine in parameters once you begin to use a variable number of arguments. If you want a quick look, jump ahead to Tip 31, *Pass a Variable Number of Arguments with the*

Rest Operator, on page 143. As you can see, the spread operator is incredibly useful and there's plenty more to explore.

Now that you've seen how it works, it's time to look at how you can rewrite common array actions using the spread operator to avoid confusing mutations and side effects.

Tip 8

Avoid Push Mutations with the Spread Operator

In this tip, you'll learn how to avoid array mutations by creating new arrays with the spread operator.

As you've just seen, mutations can have unexpected consequences. If you change something in a collection early in the code, you can create a bug much deeper. Mutations may not always cause major headaches, but they do have that potential, so it's best to avoid them when possible. In fact, some popular JavaScript libraries (such as Redux) won't allow functions with any mutations at all.

Plus, a lot of modern JavaScript is functional in style, meaning you'll need to write code that doesn't contain side effects and mutations. There's a lot to be said about functional JavaScript, more than what can fit in this book. If you're interested, you can learn more in *Functional JavaScript [Fog13]* by Michael Fogus.

I hope by now you understand why mutations are bad. But if you're like me, you probably wonder what does it all mean in practice? Consider a common array mutation: push(). The push() method changes the original array by adding an item to the end. When you add an item, you're mutating the original array. Fortunately, you can avoid the side effect with the spread operator.

Before that, start with a problem caused by the push() method.

Imagine a simple function that takes a shopping cart and summarizes the contents. The function checks to see if there are too many discounts and returns an error object if there are. Otherwise, if the cart has enough items, it adds a free gift.

```
arrays/push/push.js
const cart = [
  {
    name: 'The Foundation Triology',
    price: 19.99,
    discount: false,
  },
  {
    name: 'Godel, Escher, Bach',
    price: 15.99,
    discount: false,
  },
```

```
  {
    name: 'Red Mars',
    price: 5.99,
    discount: true,
  },
];
const reward = {
  name: 'Guide to Science Fiction',
  discount: true,
  price: 0,
};
function addFreeGift(cart) {
  if (cart.length > 2) {
    cart.push(reward);
    return cart;
  }
  return cart;
}
function summarizeCart(cart) {
  const discountable = cart.filter(item => item.discount);
  if (discountable.length > 1) {
    return {
      error: 'Can only have one discount',
    };
  }
  const cartWithReward = addFreeGift(cart);
  return {
    discounts: discountable.length,
    items: cartWithReward.length,
    cart: cartWithReward,
  };
}
```

The cart is a simple array, and the gift is merely an added item. The problem is this code is one line away from causing an error. As usual, take a moment and see if you can locate the problem.

This is a great example of why a mutation can seem so harmless. What if six months down the road, a well-meaning developer decides to clear things up by putting all the variable declarations at the top of the function?

arrays/push/push.js
```
function summarizeCartUpdated(cart) {
  const cartWithReward = addFreeGift(cart);
  const discountable = cart.filter(item => item.discount);
  if (discountable.length > 1) {
    return {
      error: 'Can only have one discount',
    };
```

```
  }
  return {
    discounts: discountable.length,
    items: cartWithReward.length,
    cart: cartWithReward,
  };
}
```

Now the bug will surface. When you use the function addFreeGift(), you're mutating the cart array. It will always have at least one discount if there are more than two items. Even though you're assigning the return value (the cart with added gift) to a new variable, you've mutated the original cart array. Any time someone has a cart with more than three items and one discount, they'll get an error.

If this had a test, maybe it would be an easy fix. If there's no test, who knows how long before customer service gets an angry email.

You might notice the problem with a lot of these examples is that the mutation happens in a separate function. Good catch! In fact, that's exactly the reason why mutations can be so dangerous. When you call a function, you should trust that it won't change any supplied values. Functions that have no side effects are called "pure" functions, and that's what you should strive to achieve.

It can be even more confusing when you return a value from a function even though you mutated the input. A developer who comes through later will likely assume that the original values haven't changed given that the return value is the one with the update. In this case, they'd be wrong. The input value was also changed.

Time to fix the problem. It's so incredibly simple—you should immediately understand why the spread operator became so popular.

arrays/push/push.js
```
function addGift(cart) {
  if (cart.length > 2) {
    return [...cart, reward];
  }
  return cart;
}

function summarizeCartSpread(cart) {
  const cartWithReward = addGift(cart);
  const discountable = cart.filter(item => item.discount);
  if (discountable.length > 1) {
    return {
      error: 'Can only have one discount',
    };
  }
```

```
  return {
    discounts: discountable.length,
    items: cartWithReward.length,
    cart: cartWithReward,
  };
}
```

All you need to do is take the current array and spread it into square brackets, tacking the newest item on at the end.

In essence, all you're doing is rewriting the contents as a list. Note that this is a brand new array so there's no way we could possibly change the original array. We're just reusing the contents to make a new array.

arrays/push/push.js
```
  const titles = ['Moby Dick', 'White Teeth'];
  const moreTitles = [...titles, 'The Conscious Mind'];
// ['Moby Dick', 'White Teeth', 'The Conscious Mind'];
```

What I love most about creating new arrays this way (and I'm sure you will, too) is that you can forget so many methods. You won't need them anymore.

Quick! How do you add a new item to the start of an array? How do you make a copy of an array? Hint: It's different than assigning the same array to a new variable. Did you have to look them up? Don't worry, I still do, too. I mean, who could remember that slice() is a function to make a copy. Here they are with the spread replacement:

arrays/push/push.js
```
// Add to beginning.
  const titles = ['Moby Dick', 'White Teeth'];
  titles.shift('The Conscious Mind');

  const moreTitles = ['Moby Dick', 'White Teeth'];
  const evenMoreTitles = ['The Conscious Mind', ...moreTitles];

  // Copy
  const toCopy = ['Moby Dick', 'White Teeth'];
  const copied = toCopy.slice();

  const moreCopies = ['Moby Dick', 'White Teeth'];
  const moreCopied = [...moreCopies];
```

And of course, to repeat a point from earlier, you're signaling your intention to return an array. Another developer may not remember that slice() creates a new array, but when they see the square brackets, they'll know exactly what they'll get.

In the next tip, you'll see how creating copies of arrays can prevent problems when you must use methods that mutate arrays, such as sort().

Tip 9

Avoid Sort Confusion with the Spread Operator

In this tip, you'll learn how to use the spread operator to sort an array multiple times while getting the same result.

You've seen by now that you can replace many mutating functions with the spread operator. What should you do when there's a function that you can't easily replace? The answer is fairly simple: Use the spread operator to create a copy of the original array, and then mutate that one.

Don't let the simplicity of the answer fool you. Mutation bugs can sneak up when you least expect them.

This comes up in applications that have tabular sorting data. If you haven't written an application that displays tabular data, wait around—I guarantee you'll do it. And the minute you create that table of tabular data, the next request you'll hear from your account or project manager is to make the table sortable.

Skip the UI components and look purely at the data and functions. You need to make an application that takes an array of staff members and sorts them either by name or years of service.

Start with an array of employees.

```
arrays/sort/sortMutate.js
const staff = [
  {
    name: 'Joe',
    years: 10,
  },
  {
    name: 'Theo',
    years: 5,
  },
  {
    name: 'Dyan',
    years: 10,
  },
];
```

Next, add a couple of custom sorting functions to sort by either name or age. If you don't understand the sort functions, don't worry. It's not necessary for this example. If interested, you can check out the sort documentation on the Mozilla Developer Network.[5]

arrays/sort/sortMutate.js
```
function sortByYears(a, b) {
  if (a.years === b.years) {
    return 0;
  }
  return a.years - b.years;
}

const sortByName = (a, b) => {
  if (a.name === b.name) {
    return 0;
  }
  return a.name > b.name ? 1 : -1;
};
```

At this point, you'd just call the sort function on the array whenever the user clicks a column heading. For example, if a user chooses to sort by years of service, the function will sort and update the array.

arrays/sort/sortMutate.js
```
staff.sort(sortByYears);

// [
//   {
//     name: 'Theo',
//     years: 5
//   },
//   {
//     name: 'Joe',
//     years: 10
//   },
//   {
//     name: 'Dyan',
//     years: 10
//   },
// ];
```

Now this is where it gets tricky. When you sorted the array, you changed it. Even though the code looks likes it's finished executing, the change is still there.

Suppose the user then sorted by user name. Again, the array mutates.

---

5. https://developer.mozilla.org/en-US/docs/Web/JavaScript/Reference/Global_Objects/Array/sort

arrays/sort/sortMutate.js

```
staff.sort(sortByName);

// [
//   {
//     name: 'Dyan',
//     years: 10
//   },
//   {
//     name: 'Joe',
//     years: 10
//   },
//   {
//     name: 'Theo',
//     years: 5
//   },
// ];
```

Nothing spectacular, but look what happens if the user goes back and sorts by years of service again. Maybe they forgot a name. Maybe they needed some different information. Who knows?

What result would the user see? What result do you *think* the user should see? Turns out, sorting by name a second time yields completely different results.

arrays/sort/sortMutate.js

```
staff.sort(sortByYears);

// [
//   {
//     name: 'Theo',
//     years: 5
//   },
//   {
//     name: 'Dyan',
//     years: 10
//   },
//   {
//     name: 'Joe',
//     years: 10
//   },
// ]
```

This is a simple example. Imagine a table of hundreds of employees with many of the employees sharing the same years of service. Every time a user clicks the sort button, they'd see a slightly different order.

At that point, your user has lost trust in the application. That's something you don't want. Mutations can have big impacts.

How do you stop mutations when the method you want to use has to mutate the data? The answer is simple: Don't mutate the data. Make a copy and then perform the mutation.

The only thing you need to change in your code is to spread the original array into a new array before sorting.

arrays/sort/sortSpread.js
```
[...staff].sort(sortByYears);

// [
//   {
//     name: 'Theo',
//     years: 5
//   },
//   {
//     name: 'Joe',
//     years: 10
//   },
//   {
//     name: 'Dyan',
//     years: 10
//   },
// ];
```

Now your users can sort however much they want because we aren't changing the original array. The results will always be the same as the previous sort for that type.

The spread operator is great, not because it's complex (you'll see some fancier collections in just a moment), but because it's so incredibly simple while still being incredibly powerful.

In the next chapter, you'll start to branch out into other collections. You'll learn when it is appropriate to use Map, Set, or standard objects.

CHAPTER 3

Maximize Code Clarity with Special Collections

I'll admit I like organizing things. I change my garage constantly. I keep all the little screws in a box with drawers that I can easily pull out. I keep most hand tools on a pegboard, but I have a couple of small toolboxes stocked with the most common items for carrying around the house to do small repairs. And I keep a few cardboard boxes full of odds and ends.

The thing is that I don't need those containers. I can (and have) stuffed everything into one cardboard box, but it certainly doesn't make my life easier. I keep things separated because the container does matter. It changes how quickly I find what I need (drawers), how easily I can identify what I have or don't have (pegboard), and how seamlessly I can transport the whole group of things around the house (toolbox).

I bet you see where this is going. This chapter is all about how to use collections to make your data easy to use and accessible. After all, the collections you use for your data can change how you work with the data.

The beauty of code is that, unlike my garage, you can switch back and forth between containers. That's great. You should always use the best collection for the job, and fortunately for you, the options in JavaScript have significantly increased.

What to do with all this new information? When choosing a variable declaration, you learned that the most important consideration was signaling intention to future developers. Similarly, when choosing a collection, you just have to ask yourself one question: how can you maintain simplicity and flexibility?

In this chapter, you'll look at different collection types and how they can give you flexibility and simplicity and when they might lead to confusing and buggy code.

You'll start off by looking at objects used as key-value collections and when they're an appropriate choice for data that won't be changed. From there, you'll see two new collections, Map and Set. You'll learn why those were introduced and how they create clear interfaces for working with data that you'll update or iterate over.

In addition, you'll learn how and when to switch over to another structure to take advantage of its methods before switching back to your original structure.

Even if you make a choice that ends up being wrong (and who among us hasn't made a few wrong choices when writing code?), you aren't going to be bound by it indefinitely. Take a look at the choices, select the one best suited to your task, but don't be afraid if you have to switch later. It's easy. The collection you use to hold your data does matter. But unlike my garage, you won't need to spend a Saturday rearranging things if you need to make a change.

Tip 10

Use Objects for Static Key-Value Lookups

In this tip, you'll learn why objects are the best collection for simple key-value lookups.

You probably noticed that I love arrays. But they are not appropriate in many situations. As you saw, it is always possible to store any type of information in arrays—they are really are that flexible—but it can make things more confusing than necessary. And you often end up obscuring information more than you communicate it.

What if you had some data and you wanted to conditionally apply some colors in the UI. You want the data to be red if data was below threshold, green if everything is within normal range, and blue if some data was above a threshold. As usual, some very smart designer with a lot of training picked the absolute perfect shades of these colors (personally, I can never tell the difference, but that's why I don't design).

You could put the hex values in an array, but that doesn't really communicate much.

```
const colors = ['#d10202', '#19d836', '#0e33d8'];
```

What the heck does #d10202 even mean? It happens to be a shade of red, but there's no way to know that without actually knowing it ahead of time. The problem is that this data is related—it's all colors—but not interchangeable. Unlike an array of users where all users are structurally similar and one can be substituted for another, the different colors will serve different purposes (indicating value to users). When a developer wants the hex code for red, they don't care what other values are in the collection. They don't need to know that red is the first or third color. In this case, a key-value collection will be more appropriate. You really need to give future developers a better idea of what the information means.

In cases where arrays aren't appropriate and you want a key-value collection, most developers reach for objects. And objects are great, but as you will see in upcoming tips, there are now more options for key-value collections.

The TC39 committee added more options for collections because objects are complex. They can be key-value collections, which is how you will use them in this chapter, or they can be closer to classes with constructors, methods, and properties. Most things in JavaScript, including other collection types, are objects at their core.

This chapter will leave aside some of the complexities of object properties, prototypes, and the keyword this and instead look at how objects are used as key-value collections. The keyword this, for example, is a huge topic that's well covered by Kyle Simpson in *You Don't Know JS: this & Object Prototypes.* [Sim14]

Now that you are thinking about objects primarily as collections competing against other collection types, such as Map, the new challenge is knowing when to chose plain objects deliberately, as the best solution for the problem, and not as a default.

As a rule, objects are great when you want to share unchanging structured key-value data, but are not appropriate for dynamic information that is updated frequently or unknown until runtime, as you will see in later tips.

For example, if you wanted to share your collection of colors, objects are a great choice. The data doesn't change. You wouldn't dynamically change the hex value for red. In this case, you can change your array of colors to an object by adding keys and wrapping the whole thing in curly braces. When you create an object this way, with key-values in curly braces, you are using object literal syntax.

```
const colors = {
    red: '#d10202',
    green: '#19d836',
    blue: '#0e33d8'
}
```

When a future developer wants to get the proper color red, they don't need to know a position; they just call it directly: colors.red. Alternatively, they can use array syntax colors['red']. It's simple. That's why objects are so valuable for retrieving static information.

The key here is static information. Objects are not good for information that's continually updated, looped over, altered, or sorted. In those cases, use Map. Objects are a path to find information when you know where it will be. Config files are often objects because they are set up before runtime and are simple key-value stores of static information.

collections/object/object.js
```
export const config = {
  endpoint: 'http://pragprog.com',
  key: 'secretkey',
};
```

But static objects can also be defined programmatically. For example, you can build an object in a function and then pass it to another function. The information is collected, sent, and then unpacked in another function. In this way, it's static because it is not mutated and updated.

The trick is that the data is set and then retrieved the *same* way *every* time. You are not mutating an existing object; you are creating a new object in each function. And more importantly, you know the key names when you are writing the code. You are not setting the keys using variables. The next function knows in advance what it will be getting.

collections/object/object.js
```
function getBill(item) {
  return {
    name: item.name,
    due: twoWeeksFromNow(),
    total: calculateTotal(item.price),
  };
}

const bill = getBill({ name: 'Room Cleaning', price: 30 });

function displayBill(bill) {
  return `Your total ${bill.total} for ${bill.name} is due on ${bill.due}`;
}
```

In the preceding example, an object is being used to add structure to information passed between objects. Instead of writing displayBill() as a function that takes each item as a parameter, you are passing the object, and the function is pulling out the values it needs.

This is where objects are far superior to other collections. Not only are they quick and clear, but with object destructuring, pulling data from objects is even quicker and cleaner than ever. Jump ahead to Tip 29, *Access Object Properties with Destructuring*, on page 133 if you want to see it in action. Destructuring is part of the reason why nothing beats an object for a quick lookup.

But again, notice that the function is creating a new object. It's setting the information and then immediately retrieving it in a different function. It's not setting the information repeatedly. If you want to add lots of information to an object programmatically, other collections may be better suited for the task, such as the Map object, which we'll explore in Tip 13, *Update Key-Value Data Clearly with Maps*, on page 54.

For now, you know that objects still play a huge role in JavaScript. You'll use them all the time when you're sharing information. In the next two tips, you'll look at a common use case: combining two similar objects together. And then you'll explore some other collections that you can use in place of objects.

Objects will come up more when you get to functions and classes, but for now, remember to keep their usage at a basic level and take a moment to consider other collections before creating an object.

In the next tip, you'll dive into working with objects, beginning with making changes to objects without mutations.

Tip 11

Create Objects Without Mutations Using Object.assign()

In this tip, you'll learn how to update an object without mutations, using Object.assign().

In the previous tip, you took a quick look at objects and got rules for when they offer distinct advantages over other collections. Still, you need to be careful when using them because they can leave you open to the same problems with mutations and side effects that you saw in arrays. Casually adding and setting fields on objects can create unseen problems.

Consider a very common problem. You have an object with a number of key-values pairs. The problem is that the object is incomplete. This happens often when you have legacy data and there are new fields, or you are getting data from an external API and you need it to match your data model. Either way, the issue is the same: you want to fill in the remaining fields using a default object.

How can you create a new object that preserves the original data while adding in the defaults? And, of course, you don't want side effects or mutations.

Take a moment to write out the code. See what you come up with.

If you wrote the code out, it would probably look something like this:

collections/assign/problem.js
```
const defaults = {
  author: '',
  title: '',
  year: 2017,
  rating: null,
};

const book = {
  author: 'Joe Morgan',
  title: 'Simplifying JavaScript',
};

function addBookDefaults(book, defaults) {
  const fields = Object.keys(defaults);
  const updated = {};
```

```
  for (let i = 0; i < fields.length; i++) {
    const field = fields[i];
    updated[field] = book[field] || defaults[field];
  }
  return updated;
}
```

There's nothing wrong with this code, but it sure is wordy. Fortunately, this was a common enough issue that ES5 introduced Object.assign() to create and update fields on an object with keys and values from another object (or objects).

In other words, Object.assign() lets you update an object with properties from another object.

So how does Object.assign() work? It's fairly simple. The method takes a series of objects and updates the inner-most object with the keys and values from outer objects, then returns the updated first object. The outermost object has precedence over any inner objects.

It's easier to see than explain, but when you see how simple it is, you'll love it. Here's how you can rewrite addBookDefaults() using Object.assign():

collections/assign/mutate.js
```
Object.assign(defaults, book);

// {
//    author: 'Joe Morgan',
//    title: 'Simplifying JavaScript',
//    year: 2017,
//    rating: null,
// }
```

Your nine-line function dropped to a single line. But by now, you may have guessed there's a problem in this code. When it updates the initial object—the default object—it also mutates the original. If you run the code again with a different book object, you'll get an unexpected result.

collections/assign/mutate.js
```
const anotherBook = {
  title: 'Another book',
  year: 2016,
};

Object.assign(defaults, anotherBook);

// {
//    author: 'Joe Morgan',
//    title: 'Simplifying JavaScript',
//    year: 2017,
//    rating: null,
// }
```

You accidentally changed the default object to make me, 'Joe', the default author, so I'm going to start getting credit for a whole bunch of books I've never written.

Fortunately, the solution is simple. Just make the first object an empty object. After you do that, the returned object will be the updated empty object. The other objects will have no mutations.

```
collections/assign/assign.js
const defaults = { author: '',
  title: '',
  year: 2017,
  rating: null,
};

const book = {
  author: 'Joe Morgan',
  title: 'Simplifying JavaScript',
};

const updated = Object.assign({}, defaults, book);
```

Now, there's one problem with copying objects using Object.assign(). When it copies over properties, it just copies the values. That may seem like it's not a problem, but it is.

Up to this point, you've been working with flat objects. Every key had a simple value: a string or an integer. And when all you have is a series of strings or integers, it copies them just fine, as you saw earlier. But when the value is another object, you start to have problems.

```
collections/assign/assign.js
const defaultEmployee = {
  name: {
    first: '',
    last: '',
  },
  years: 0,
};

const employee = Object.assign({}, defaultEmployee);
```

Copying objects that have nested objects is called "deep copying" (or "deep merging" or some variation). The property years will copy over just fine, but the property name isn't copied. All that's copied is a reference to the independent object that's assigned to the key name. The nested object essentially exists independently of the object that holds it. All the containing object has is a reference to that object. When you copy the reference, you aren't making a deep copy of the nested object. You're merely copying the location of the reference.

So if you change a value of a nested object on either the original or the copy, it will change the value on both.

collections/assign/assign.js
```
employee.name.first = 'Joe';

defaultEmployee;

// {
//    name: {
//       first:'Joe',
//       last: '',
//    },
//    years: 0
// }
```

There are two ways around this problem: The first and simplest is to keep your objects flat—don't have nested objects if you can avoid it.

Unfortunately, that doesn't work in a situation where you start off with a nested object. Maybe the software was designed with nested objects. Maybe you're getting a result from an API that's nested. It doesn't matter. Nested objects are very common.

In that case, you can copy the nested objects with Object.assign(); you just need a little more code. Whenever there is a nested object, copy that with Object.assign() and everything will be updated.

collections/assign/assign.js
```
const employee2 = Object.assign(
  {},
  defaultEmployee,
  {
    name: Object.assign({}, defaultEmployee.name),
  },
);

export { defaults };
```

Of course, there are other options: A library like Lodash has a method called cloneDeep() that can do this for you. And by all means, take advantage of community libraries, but sometimes you may want to make a change without external code.

If you're thinking that code is getting ugly fast, you're not wrong. It feels like it could be simpler. Sure, you can abstract it out into a helper function, but fortunately, you may not even need to do that. There's experimental syntax that, though not adopted, is widely used throughout the JavaScript community and will likely be part of the official spec soon. The best part is, it looks exactly like something you've already seen. It's called the Object Spread operator, and it will give you the ability to make new objects with the now familiar spread operator.

In the next tip, you'll learn how use the new syntax to update object information quickly and clearly.

Tip 12

Update Information with Object Spread

In this tip, you'll learn how the object spread operator gives you all the advantages of Object.assign() with reduced syntax.

You saw in the previous tip how you can use Object.assign() to make copies of objects and how you can overwrite object values with new values from another object. It's a great tool that has a lot of value. But, wow—it's ugly.

The spread operator was such a popular addition in ES6 that similar syntax is being introduced for objects. The object spread operator is not officially part of the spec, but it's so widely used that it will likely be adopted in the future. You can check out the proposal on github.[1]

Using Proposed Syntax

JavaScript developers love new syntax. In fact, they love it so much they often start using it before it's officially adopted. This is the case with the object spread operator and other things such as private methods in classes. You see them in many code bases even though the spec is not official.

Deciding when to use proposed syntax is a matter of preference. I tend to be pretty conservative and only adopt proposed syntax when it's very clear that the community supports the change and the proposal is unlikely to change.

Once you decide to use proposed syntax, you will need to make a few changes to your development environment. If you use Babel for compiling your code in order to be compatible across browsers, all you have to do is add a plugin and everything works fine. If you are on Node.js, it can be a little more difficult. Many features are supported using the --harmony flag when starting Node.js.

Feel free to experiment, but be aware you may need to refactor code if the official proposal changes.

How does the object spread operator work? Well, it's simple. It works like the array spread operator—the key-values are returned as if in a list. You can easily add information by placing it either before or after the spread. And like the array spread, you must spread it out into something.

---

1. https://github.com/tc39/proposal-object-rest-spread

```
collections/objectSpread/objectSpread.js
const book = {
  title: 'Reasons and Persons',
  author: 'Derek Parfit',
};

const update = { ...book, year: 1984 };

// { title: 'Reasons and Persons', author: 'Derek Parfit', year: 1984}
```

But it's different from the array spread in that if you add a value with the same key, it will use whatever value is declared last.

In this way, it's like Object.assign() with much less typing.

```
collections/objectSpread/objectSpread.js
const book = {
  title: 'Reasons and Persons',
  author: 'Derek Parfit',
};

const update = { ...book, title: 'Reasons & Persons' };

// { title: 'Reasons & Persons', author: 'Derek Parfit' }
```

That's it! It takes the best existing features and combines them. You will not be surprised to learn that the JavaScript community embraces it enthusiastically.

Now that you have some great new syntax, try rewriting the functions from the previous tip. I'll give you the original and then the updated version. But try it yourself. It's very simple.

Here's the way to add or update information with Object.assign():

```
collections/assign/assign.js
const defaults = { author: '',
  title: '',
  year: 2017,
  rating: null,
};

const book = {
  author: 'Joe Morgan',
  title: 'Simplifying JavaScript',
};

const updated = Object.assign({}, defaults, book);
```

And here it is with the object spread operator:

```
collections/objectSpread/objectSpread.js
const defaults = {
  author: '',
  title: '',
  year: 2017,
  rating: null,
};

const book = {
  author: 'Joe Morgan',
  title: 'ES6 Tips',
};

const bookWithDefaults = { ...defaults, ...book };

// {
//    author: 'Joe Morgan',
//    title: 'ES6 Tips',
//    year: 2017,
//    rating: null,
// }
```

You'll have the same deep merge problems that you have with Object.assign():
you don't copy nested objects—you only copy a reference creating a potential
problem with mutations.

Fortunately, the fix is less painful on the eyes. Here's the original.

```
collections/assign/assign.js
const employee2 = Object.assign(
  {},
  defaultEmployee,
  {
    name: Object.assign({}, defaultEmployee.name),
  },
);

export { defaults };
```

Now, before you the look at the answer, really try this out. It's straightforward,
but still a little more complex. Got it? Okay. Here's the same update with the
object spread operator.

```
collections/objectSpread/objectSpread.js
const employee = {
  ...defaultEmployee,
  name: {
    ...defaultEmployee.name,
  },
};
```

The advantages are clear. The code is more readable. You're signaling your intention to create an object in a clear way. You don't have to worry about mutations because you don't need to remember to start with an empty object.

The object spread is fantastic—it's great for your code and gives you an opportunity to integrate experimental features in your code base.

That's all there is for existing collections. In the next tip, you will finally get to try out some completely new collections that should improve your code communication. First up, the Map object.

Tip 13

Update Key-Value Data Clearly with Maps

In this tip, you'll learn how to use the Map object for key-value collections of frequently updated data.

In Tip 10, *Use Objects for Static Key-Value Lookups*, on page 41, you learned that you should only use objects deliberately and not as a default collection. Now you're going to get a chance to look at an alternative: Map.

Map is a special kind of collection that can do certain things very easily. The Mozilla Developer Network has a nice list of circumstances where Map is a better option for a collection than a plain object.[2] I encourage you to read the full list, but this tip examines two specific situations:

- Key-value pairs are frequently added or removed.
- A key isn't a string.

In the next tip, you'll see another big advantage: using Map for iterating over collections. For now, you just need to be familiar with adding or removing values to maps.

First, think about what it means that key-value pairs are frequently added and removed. Consider a pet adoption website. The site has a list of all the adorable dogs that need homes. Because people have different expectations of their pets (some want big dogs, some like certain breeds), you'll need to include a way to filter the animals.

You'll start off with a collection of animals:

```
const dogs = [
  {
    name: 'max',
    size: 'small',
    breed: 'boston terrier',
    color: 'black'
  },
  {
    name: 'don',
    size: 'large',
    breed: 'labrador',
```

---

2.   https://developer.mozilla.org/en-US/docs/Web/JavaScript/Reference/Global_Objects/Map

```
    color: 'black'
  },
  {
    name: 'shadow',
    size: 'medium',
    breed: 'labrador',
    color: 'chocolate'
  }
]
```

The collection of all dogs is an array, which makes sense because the shape of each item in the collection is the same.

You'll need to create one more collection: your list of applied filters. The filters will be a collection containing a key (color) and a value (black). The user will need to be able to add a filter, remove a filter, and clear all filter values.

If you added the key "color" and the value "black" to the collection, then somewhere else in the code base, you'll filter the objects using that information and be left with an array of two dogs. Don't worry about the implementation details. But if you're curious, take a look at Tip 23, *Pull Out Subsets of Data with filter() and find()*, on page 102 to see how to filter an array.

To understand why Map was added to the spec, think of how you might solve the problem with standard objects.

First, you'd make an empty object that will hold the new information:

```
let filters = {};
```

Then you'd need three actions to update the information on the object: add filter, remove a filter, clear all filters.

collections/map/problem.js
```
function addFilters(filters, key, value) {
  filters[key] = value;
}

function deleteFilters(filters, key) {
  delete filters[key];
}

function clearFilters(filters) {
  filters = {};
  return filters;
}
```

The strange thing here is even though you're performing three basic actions on a collection—setting a key-value, deleting a key-value, clearing all key-values—you're using three different paradigms. The first, setting a key-value, uses a method on the object itself. The second, deleting a key-value pair, uses an operator defined by the language. The third, clearing all data, reassigns a variable. It's not even an action on the object. It's variable reassignment. When you "clear" an object, you're really just writing `filters = new Object();`.

By contrast, maps are designed specifically to update key-value pairs frequently. The interface is clear, methods have predictable names, and actions such as loops (as you'll see in the next tip) are built in. This will make you a more productive developer. The more you can predict, the faster you can create.

Browser Engines

JavaScript code has to be interpreted by an engine but, complicating the process, there are many different engines. The most popular is the V8 engine, which powers Chrome and Node. But there's also SpiderMonkey (Firefox) and Chakra (Internet Explorer/Edge). Features can be implemented in different ways. And some syntax changes have advantages beyond code clarity.

Because maps are a more specialized collection, the developers of JavaScript engines can optimize the code to make actions faster. Key lookups for objects will be linear, but when maps are implemented natively, their lookup time can be logarithmic.[a]

In other words, big objects are more expensive than big maps.

You can see some projects, such as React, switching to natively implemented maps purely for performance reasons.[b] You'll likely never need to make a choice between objects or maps for performance reasons, but it's good to know that the underlying engines do treat them differently.

---

a.　https://developer.mozilla.org/en-US/docs/Web/JavaScript/Data_structures#Keyed_collections_Maps_Sets_WeakMaps_WeakSets

b.　https://github.com/facebook/react/pull/7232#issuecomment-231516712

To begin, you need to create a new instance of `Map` and add some data.

Unlike an object, which has a simple constructor shortcut using curly braces, you must always explicitly create a new instance of a `Map`.

```
let filters = new Map();
```

Notice that you assigned the new map with `let`. `let` is a better choice because you'll be mutating the object by adding some data. You may be a little confused. After spending a lot of time learning how mutations are bad, here's an object that, by necessity, must be mutated whenever you add or remove data. For now, don't worry about the mutations. There is a way around mutating the object, and you'll see it in the next tip.

After creating an instance, you add data with the set() method. To add a breed of 'labrador' to the filter list, you'd pass in the key name 'breed' as the first argument and the value 'labrador' as the second argument.

```
filters.set('breed', 'labrador');
```

To retrieve date, use the get() method, passing in the key as the only argument.

```
filters.get('breed');
// labrador
```

Getting and setting data is simple, but it can be tedious for a large map. Fortunately, the creators of the spec anticipated this and created a few shortcuts when setting data.

You can easily add several values with chaining—applying methods one after the other. You can even chain directly from the creation of the new instance. You'll see more about chaining methods in Tip 25, *Combine Methods with Chaining*, on page 110.

```
let filters = new Map()
  .set('breed', 'labrador')
  .set('size', 'large')
  .set('color', 'chocolate');

filters.get('size');
// 'large'
```

That's not the only way you can add data. You can also add information using an array.

Remember in Tip 5, *Create Flexible Collections with Arrays*, on page 19, you learned that key-value objects can be represented as an array of pairs. Here's a perfect use case. Instead of creating a new Map and then chaining setters, you can pass an array of pairs with the first element being a key and the second element being a value.

```
let filters = new Map(
    [
        ['breed', 'labrador'],
        ['size', 'large'],
        ['color', 'chocolate'],
    ]
)

filters.get('color');
// 'chocolate'
```

If you want to remove values, you just need to use the delete() method rather than the language operator.

```
filters.delete('color');
```

```
filters.get('color');
// undefined
```

Similarly, you can delete all the key-value pairs with the clear() method.

```
filters.clear()
```

```
filters.get('color');
// undefined
```

With these methods outlined, you have the foundation to change your functions to use a map instead of an object.

```
collections/map/map.js
const petFilters = new Map();
function addFilters(filters, key, value) {
  filters.set(key, value);
}

function deleteFilters(filters, key) {
  filters.delete(key);
}

function clearFilters(filters) {
  filters.clear();
}
```

The change is subtle but very important. First, the code is much cleaner. That's a big advantage in itself. But you'll see far bigger advantages when you compare these functions to the ones you created with an object. With these functions:

- You always use a method on a Map instance.
- You don't mix in language operators after you create the initial instance.
- You don't ever have to create a new instance to perform a simple action.

These are the reasons why maps are so much easier to work with than objects when you're frequently changing the information. Every action and intention is very clear.

In addition, with objects you're limited in the types of keys you can use. Objects can use only certain types of keys. Most significantly, you can't use integers as a string, which causes problems if you want to store information by a numerical ID. For example, if you have an object of error codes:

```
const errors = {
  100: 'Invalid name',
  110: 'Name should only contain letters',
  200: 'Invalid color'
};
```

you may innocently think you could retrieve error text by the numerical code.

```
function isDataValid(data) {
  if(data.length < 10) {
    return errors.100
  }
  return true;
}
```

This code would throw an Error. Integers as keys can't be accessed with dot syntax. You're still able to access the information using array notation errors[100]. But that's actually a bit of a trick. You get the right result because when you created the error array, it converted all the integers to strings. And when you use array syntax, it's also converting the integer to a string before lookup. If you tried to get the keys, it would return an array of strings:

```
Object.keys(errors);
// ['100', '110', '200']
```

A Map wouldn't have that problem. It can take many different types as keys.

```
let errors = new Map([
    [100, 'Invalid name'],
    [110, 'Name should only contain letters'],
    [200, 'Invalid color']
]);

errors.get(100);
// 'Invalid name'
}
```

In case you're wondering, you can also get the keys from a Map as you could with an object.

```
errors.keys();

// MapIterator { 100, 110, 200 }
}
```

Notice something strange? When you asked for the keys, you didn't get an array, as you do with Object.keys(). You didn't get an object, or even another Map; the return value is something called MapIterator. Don't worry—it's actually a great thing to have. The MapIterator is what will allow us to loop through data.

In the next tip, you'll see how the MapIterator is the killer feature that will make you return to Map over and over again.

Tip 14

Iterate Over Key-Value Data with Map and the Spread Operator

In this tip, you'll learn how to iterate directly over key-value data in maps with either loops or the spread operator.

In the previous tip, you saw how maps are an improved key-value collection when you're regularly adding or deleting items. As you saw, objects are very useful, but there are times when a map has distinct advantages. You can see those advantages on the Mozilla Developer Network.[3]

You've already explored several advantages pertaining to when keys are set. Now you're going to explore another suggested usage for maps: collections that are iterated.

Objects are very frustrating to iterate over. In fact, there used to be no way to directly iterate over them. You were always forced to transform them before you could loop over the data. Things are a little better. You can now use a for...in loop to iterate over objects, but you'll have access only to the object key. In a way, it's not much different from looping over an array of keys. Check out Tip 27, *Reduce Loop Clutter with for...in and for...each*, on page 120 for more about the for...in loop.

As you can see. Looping over objects is complicated. Conversely, you can iterate over maps directly.

Start by returning to your filters. Suppose you have an object of filters and you want to list the applied filters. After all, you want your users to remember they're seeing a subset of information. How would you write code that translates the objects to a string?

How would you, for example, transform all the key-values to be a string of the form "key:value"?

The odd thing is you won't iterate over the filters object. Instead, you'll pull out other information and then iterate over that.

---

3. https://developer.mozilla.org/en-US/docs/Web/JavaScript/Reference/Global_Objects/Map

collections/mapSpread/object.js
```
const filters = {
  color: 'black',
  breed: 'labrador',
};

function getAppliedFilters(filters) {
  const keys = Object.keys(filters);
  const applied = [];
  for (const key of keys) {
    applied.push(`${key}:${filters[key]}`);
  }
  return `Your filters are: ${applied.join(', ')}.`;
}
// 'Your filters are: color:black, breed:labrador.'
```

Looking at the code, you see that the first step is pulling out a section of the object into an array with Object.keys() and then you iterate over the keys with a for loop. And during that for loop, you have to pull the value out by referencing the object again.

Plus, there's no guarantee of order in an object. That means an object can't be sorted. If you wanted to get the filters in sorted order, you'd first need to sort the keys.

collections/mapSpread/object.js
```
function getSortedAppliedFilters(filters) {
  const keys = Object.keys(filters);
  keys.sort();
  const applied = [];
  for (const key of keys) {
    applied.push(`${key}:${filters[key]}`);
  }
  return `Your filters are: ${applied.join(', ')}.`;
}
// 'Your filters are: breed:labrador, color:black.'
```

That's a lot to keep track of when you want to do a simple iteration. A Map, by contrast, has everything you need to sort and iterate built in as part of the MapIterator you saw at the end of the previous tip.

To begin exploring the MapIterator, look at a simple for loop on your filters map. The for ... of syntax is also fairly new, but it's very simple. It returns each value in the collection one at a time. You'll explore it a little more in Tip 27, *Reduce Loop Clutter with for...in and for...each*, on page 120.

```
collections/mapSpread/iterate.js
const filters = new Map()
  .set('color', 'black')
  .set('breed', 'labrador');

function checkFilters(filters) {
  for (const entry of filters) {
    console.log(entry);
  }
}
// ['color', 'black']
// ['breed', 'labrador']
```

A few things should have immediately jumped out to you. The item you get from the iterator is neither the key nor the value. It's not even another Map. It's a pair of the key-value.

Even though you created this map using the set() method, it still translated the information back to an array. You also used a specific variable name, entries(), because Map has a special method that will give you a MapIterator of the key-values of a map as a group of pairs:

```
filters.entries();
// MapIterator { [ 'color', 'black' ], [ 'breed', 'labrador' ] }
```

Keep that in mind—you'll return to it in a moment. For now, just understand that a simple loop on a map will give you both the keys and the values in a pair. In fact, the ability to get entries is so convenient that it's being added to a method on objects in the next version of the JavaScript spec.[4]

Of course, that means you'll be able to apply all the ideas you learn here to objects directly in the near future. That's another good reason to experiment with maps even if you don't adopt them often.

Return to your original method for turning key-values into a string using a for loop. Because you can iterate directly over the map, you don't need to pull out the keys first. Plus, when you loop over the entries in a map, you get a pair of the key-values, which you can immediately assign to variables using destructuring. You'll explore this more in Tip 29, *Access Object Properties with Destructuring*, on page 133.

The result is more simple, and it helps you avoid breaking apart your data structure.

---

4. https://github.com/tc39/proposal-object-values-entries

collections/mapSpread/iterate.js
```
function getAppliedFilters(filters) {
  const applied = [];
  for (const [key, value] of filters) {
    applied.push(`${key}:${value}`);
  }
  return `Your filters are: ${applied.join(', ')}.`;
}
// 'Your filters are: color:black, breed:labrador.'
```

Of course, you quickly realize that you have the same sorting problem as you did earlier. Well, there is good news and bad news for you: The good news is that Map *does* preserve order. The first item you have will always be the first item in the map. The bad news is that there isn't a built-in sort method as there is for an array.

In other words, you can't do this:

```
filters.sort()
```

All of a sudden, your map is looking less helpful. Fortunately, there's a very simple solution: the spread operator.

The spread operator works on a map the same way it does on an array. The main difference is that it returns a list of pairs instead of single values.

```
...filters;
// ['color', 'black'], ['breed', 'labrador']
```

And like the spread operator on arrays, you have to spread it into something, which means you can easily make an array of pairs:

```
[...filters];
// [['color', 'black'], ['breed', 'labrador']]
```

I hope this has given you an idea about how to solve your sort problem. Try it out and see what you come up with. The only catch is that, because you're sorting an array of arrays, you should supply an explicit compare function. This isn't strictly necessary because the default compare function will convert the array of pairs to a string, but it's better to be clear in your intentions. Once you learn how to make arrow functions in Tip 20, *Simplify Looping with Arrow Functions*, on page 89, the compare function will be a one liner.

I bet you came up with something simple like this.

collections/mapSpread/iterate.js
```
function sortByKey(a, b) {
  return a[0] > b[0] ? 1 : -1;
}

function getSortedAppliedFilters(filters) {
  const applied = [];
  for (const [key, value] of [...filters].sort(sortByKey)) {
    applied.push(`${key}:${value}`);
  }
  return `Your filters are: ${applied.join(', ')}.`;
}
// 'Your filters are: breed:labrador, color:black.'
```

Now look closely—it can be easy to miss. In the for loop initiator when you're assigning variables, you quickly spread the map out into an array and then sorted that array. Now you're getting the results you wanted.

There's a slight problem. If you read the code carefully, you may have noticed that something changed. You started off with a map, but your for loop didn't actually iterate over the map. It iterated over a new array.

Honestly, this isn't much of a problem. There's nothing wrong with converting to an array. In fact, it gives you an opportunity to simplify your function even more.

Now that you can move easily to an array, you might as well use all of the array methods at your disposal. Because you're changing every value of the array in the same way, you don't need to create a new array to collect the results as you did with let applied = []. You can simply use the map() method. If that's new to you, jump ahead to Tip 22, *Create Arrays of a Similar Size with map()*, on page 98. Try rewriting your initial function to use the map() method.

collections/mapSpread/mapSpread.js
```
function getAppliedFilters(filters) {
  const applied = [...filters].map(([key, value]) => {
    return `${key}:${value}`;
  });
  return `Your filters are: ${applied.join(', ')}.`;
}
// 'Your filters are: color:black, breed:labrador.'
```

And because everything is now an array, you can combine your sort() function and your join() function using chaining to get everything nice and simple.

collections/mapSpread/mapSpread.js

```
function getSortedAppliedFilters(filters) {
  const applied = [...filters]
    .sort(sortByKey)
    .map(([key, value]) => {
      return `${key}:${value}`;
    })
    .join(', ');

  return `Your filters are: ${applied}.`;
}
// 'Your filters are: breed:labrador, color:black.'
```

If you're getting lost, here's a summary of the steps:

1. Convert your map to an array.

2. Sort the array.

3. Convert each pair to a string of the form key:value.

4. Join the array items creating a string.

5. Combine the string with other information using a template literal.

It's worth repeating that a strong knowledge of arrays can help you create very simple and efficient code. Now that you know that you can move between a map and array with three simple dots, you've opened yourself up to many more opportunities for creatively using maps.

In the next tip, you'll see how you can use the spread operator to avoid side effects and mutations.

Create Maps Without Side Effects

In this tip, you'll learn how to avoid side effects by creating new maps from an array of pairs.

Up to this point, you've always worked on a single instance of a map. You've either added data or removed data directly from an instance of a Map object.

Working on the instance of a map can lead to a few problems. How do you create copies of a map? How can you make changes without side effects?

Fortunately, you can solve those problems by applying a few principles you've learned from arrays and objects.

To start, look at an example that combines the problems of copying and mutations: applying a set of defaults to a map.

In your pet adoption code, you have filters that users have selected, but perhaps you want to add a set of default filters. Any additional filters will be overridden by the user, but any not explicitly set by the user will be the default.

collections/mapSideEffects/sideEffects.js
```
const defaults = new Map()
  .set('color', 'brown')
  .set('breed', 'beagle')
  .set('state', 'kansas');

const filters = new Map()
  .set('color', 'black');
```

Now you're in a bind. How can you make a new collection of filters, including the defaults and the user-applied filters?

If you didn't care about side effects (and I really hope you do by now), you might be tempted to check to see if the map has a key using the has() method. If no key exists, set the key value. If the key already exists, you can ignore it.

collections/mapSideEffects/sideEffects.js
```
function applyDefaults(map, defaults) {
  for (const [key, value] of defaults) {
    if (!map.has(key)) {
      map.set(key, value);
    }
```

```
    }
  }
export { applyDefaults };
```

If your goal is solely to combine defaults and user data, you've succeeded. But by now, your skepticism about mutations should get to you. Consider how you want to use the filters object. You use it to filter data, but you also use it to alert the user to the filters they've applied (as you did by creating a string in the previous tip).

Now that you've mutated the object, it will appear to the user that they applied a bunch of defaults they never selected. Notice that the defaults include a state. You want your users to see only the animals in their state, but you don't want them to change the state directly. You'd rather they visit the pet adoption page for that state.

The simplest way around this problem is to create a copy of the map. As you may recall, you can create a new map by passing in an array of pairs. And you can create a list of pairs with the spread operator.

With that in mind, try to update the code to create a copy before it's mutated.

```
collections/mapSideEffects/copy.js
function applyDefaults(map, defaults) {
  const copy = new Map([...map]);
  for (const [key, value] of defaults) {
    if (!copy.has(key)) {
      copy.set(key, value);
    }
  }
  return copy;
}
```

If you got something like this, great work! You got the copy of the filters, and you applied the defaults to that (note that it's okay to mutate something that's scoped to the function), and then you returned the new map. Now you can be sure that your current filters map is safe from side effects while your new map contains all the defaults and all the applied information.

Yet it gets even better. You're still manually checking a bunch of keys for existence. Fortunately, that's not even necessary. Maps, like objects, can only have a key once. So if you tried to create a map with a new key, it will use whatever value for that key is declared last. It's as if you were updating the value instead of setting it.

```
const filters = new Map()
.set('color', 'black')
.set('color', 'brown');

filters.get('color');
// brown
```

With this knowledge, you can combine what you know about the object spread operator to create a combination of two maps in one line.

```
let filters = new Map()
.set('color', 'black');

let filters2 = new Map()
.set('color', 'brown');

let update =  new Map([...filters, ...filters2]);

update.get('color');

// brown
```

Now when you update the function again, you realize you don't even need the function at all. Combining and creating maps becomes a one liner.

collections/mapSideEffects/map.js

```
function applyDefaults(map, defaults) {
    return new Map([...defaults, ...map]);
}
```

Maps really do combine some of the best ideas from many other data structures. This should give you some ideas for how you can start using them in your code.

In the next tip, you'll learn about another new collection, Set, which does one thing very well: creating a list of unique items.

Tip 16

Keep Unique Values with Set

In this tip, you'll learn how to quickly pull unique items from an array with Set.

Set is a fairly simple collection that can do only one thing, but it does it very well. Set is like a specialized array that can contain only one instance of each unique item. You'll often want to collect values from a large array of objects, but you only need to know the unique values. There are other use cases as well, but collecting a list of distinct information from a group of objects is very, very common.

In that spirit, return once again to our set of filters that you're building. To even know what a user can filter on, you need to gather all the possible values. Recall the array of dogs that you worked with earlier.

```
const dogs = [
  {
    name: 'max',
    size: 'small',
    breed: 'boston terrier',
    color: 'black'
  },
  {
    name: 'don',
    size: 'large',
    breed: 'labrador',
    color: 'black'
  },
  {
    name: 'shadow',
    size: 'medium',
    breed: 'labrador',
    color: 'chocolate'
  }
]
```

How would you get a list of all the color options? In this case, the answer is obvious, but what if the list grows into several hundred dogs? How can you be sure we get all the potential choices from golden retrievers to blue pit bulls to mottled border collies?

One simple way to get a collection of all the colors is to use the map() array method. You'll explore this more in Tip 22, *Create Arrays of a Similar Size with map()*, on page 98, but for now, all you need to know is that it will return an array of only the colors.

collections/set/unique.js
```
function getColors(dogs) {
  return dogs.map(dog => dog.color);
}

getColors(dogs);

// ['black', 'black', 'chocolate']
```

The problem is that this is only the first part. Now that you have all the colors, you need to reduce that to an array of unique values. You could pull those out in a number of different ways. There are for loops and reduce() functions. But for now, stick with a simple for loop.

collections/set/unique.js
```
function getUnique(attributes) {
  const unique = [];
  for (const attribute of attributes) {
    if (!unique.includes(attribute)) {
      unique.push(attribute);
    }
  }
  return unique;
}

const colors = getColors(dogs);
getUnique(colors);
// ['black', 'chocolate']
```

Seems easy enough, but fortunately now you don't even need to write that much code. You can use the Set object to handle the work of pulling out unique values. A set is a common data type and you may be familiar with it from other languages.

The interface is very simple and resembles Map in many ways. The main difference is that instead of taking an array of pairs, you can create a new instance of Set by passing a flat array as an argument.

If you pass your array of colors into a set, you're nearly there.

```
const colors = ['black', 'black', 'chocolate'];

const unique = new Set(colors);
// Set {'black', 'chocolate'}
```

You probably noticed that the value of the object is a Set containing only one instance of each color. And that may seem like a problem. You don't want a Set—you want an array of unique items.

Well, by now you may have guessed the solution: the spread operator. You can use the spread operator on Set much like you did with Map. The only difference is that Set returns an array. Exactly what you want! Now you can refactor the getUnique() function to a one liner. Notice that you can even use the spread operator on instance creation—you don't even need to assign it to a variable.

```
collections/set/set.js
function getUnique(attributes) {
  return [...new Set(attributes)];
}
```

Maybe this code still doesn't sit well with you. Good! That means your intuition is sharpening. If it seems like you're being inefficient, you're correct. You're first looping over the array of dogs to get an array of colors; then you're manipulating that array to get a list of unique values. Can't you do both at once?

You sure can. Set, again, is similar to Map in that you have methods to add and check for values. For a set, you can add a value with add() and check a value with has(). You also have delete() and clear(), which work exactly as they do in Map.

This all means means that you can add items to a set individually as you go through a loop instead of all at once by passing an array of values. A set can keep only one of each value. If you try to add a value that isn't yet in the set, it will be added. If you try to add a value that already exists, it will be ignored. Order is preserved, and the initial point a value is added will remain. If you try to add an item that's there already, it keeps the original position.

```
let names = new Set();
names.add('joe');
// Set { 'joe'}

names.add('bea');
// Set { 'joe', 'bea'}

names.add('joe');
// Set { 'joe', 'bea'}
```

You now have the tools to get the unique values in one pass through the array of dogs. There's no need to first get all colors and then get all the unique items. You can get them in one loop.

collections/set/set.js
```
function getUniqueColors(dogs) {
  const unique = new Set();
  for (const dog of dogs) {
    unique.add(dog.color);
  }
  return [...unique];
}
```

In this code, you used a simple for loop. But you can easily simplify this action to a one liner with a reduce() function. Reduce functions are awesome and you'll love them, but they're a little more complicated. You'll get a chance to explore them thoroughly in Tip 26, *Transform Array Data with reduce()*, on page 114, but here's a sample of how you can get the unique values in one line.

collections/set/set.js
```
[...dogs.reduce((colors, { color }) => colors.add(color), new Set())];
```

By now you're probably feeling excited about all the new ways you can experiment with collections in your code. There are a few more you haven't touched, such as WeakMap and WeakSet, and you should try them out. The best place for JavaScript documentation is always The Mozilla Developer Network.[5]

But that's enough talk about collections. It's time to start building things. The next step is learning to use control structures to handle conditional actions.

In the next chapter, you'll look at how you can apply the same standards of simplicity and readability to conditional statements.

---

5.   https://developer.mozilla.org

CHAPTER 4

Write Clear Conditionals

Have you ever been sucked into a round of spring cleaning? I don't mean the kind where you put "Scrub the floors" on your to-do list and then you actually do it. Rather, say it's a nice day so you open the window, but as soon as you do, a pile of papers blows off your desk. That's fine, you've been meaning to organize those anyway. So you start filing, but without that stack of papers hiding everything, now you notice that your computer cables look all tangled and sloppy, and how long has that coffee mug been hiding back there? Before you know it, you're taking your whole office apart. Once you start removing clutter, it's hard to stop.

By now, you've likely started getting a taste for clean and simple JavaScript. And that's wonderful. The new syntax allows you to do so much more with much less code. But you don't need to wait for new syntax before you make a positive change to your code.

Let's take a quick detour from new syntax to explore some older ideas, but with a new goal: making clean and predictable JavaScript code.

In this chapter, you're going to clean up conditional expressions. You'll revisit basic ideas, such as truthy and falsy values, ternary expressions, and short circuiting, with the goal of keeping everything simple and clean.

There's also a practical side: Now that you have more tools to assign and work with data, you can reuse old ideas to further leverage the new syntax.

Here's a basic example: Let's say you wanted to set the color on a value. If the value is a negative number, you want the color to be red. If the value is positive, you want it to be green.

```
const transactions = [...spending, ...income];
const balance = calculateBalance(transactions);

let color;
```

```
if(balance > 0) {
    color = 'green';
} else {
    color = 'red';
}
```

The first two lines are like my newly cleaned desk. They're clear and expressive, and are assigned with const, so you know they aren't changing. But as with spring cleaning, you look down and suddenly things seem awfully messy.

Where did that let come from? Oh, right. You need it to set the color, which will be mutated by the conditional. I guess it's okay, but it just doesn't feel as clean as the rest of the code.

All of a sudden, that block of code just doesn't look right. Fortunately, you don't need to leave it like that. You can rewrite it with the same simple syntax as before. No new syntax necessary.

To start off, you'll look at truthy and falsy values in JavaScript. Many techniques to simplify code involve truthy and falsy values, so you'll want a firm foundation. Next, you'll look at ternaries, a simple method for reducing if/else conditionals to a single line. Finally, you'll learn to write extremely concise conditionals and variable assignment with short circuiting.

It's time to clean up the clutter in your conditionals. Between truthy values, ternaries, and short circuiting, you'll be writing conditionals that fit with your modern JavaScript code. And as you move into array methods and functions, you'll see these ideas return over and over.

Let's get started putting your house in order.

Tip 17

Shorten Conditionals with Falsy Values

In this tip, you'll learn how to use falsy and truthy values to check for information from different types.

Can you remember the first line of code you ever wrote? I can't, but I wouldn't be surprised if it was some sort of conditional. Responding one way to some information and a different way to other information is about as basic as programming can get.

I still write a lot of conditionals every day, and I bet you do, too. Fortunately, JavaScript, along with many other languages, gives you many tools for checking information and reassigning or standardizing information very quickly with minimal code.

The secret to being able to check values quickly is to understand the subtle difference between the primitive values true and false (also called Boolean types) and the many so-called truthy and falsy values—values that aren't identical to the Boolean values true or false but act like they are in most cases.

I bet you thought we were about to dig into that idea. Well, give me just one more moment to review another concept: equivalency and identity—a value that's equivalent if it's the same, but of a different type and is checked with '=='.

```
1 == '1' // true
```

Identical values, or values with strict equality, mean that they must be of the same type.

```
1 === '1' // false
1 === 1 // true
```

Objects, including instances of arrays, are checked by their reference (remember reference from Object.assign()?).

The topic can get much deeper, but for now we want to identify values that are equivalent to false or true but not identical.

Okay. Back to truthy and falsy values. An empty string is equal to false (but not identical). In other words, it's falsy.

```
'' == false // true
if('') {
    return 'I am not false!'
} else {
    return 'I am false :( !'
}
// I am false :(
```

Here's a quick list of values that are falsy courtesy of Mozilla Developer Network:[1]

- false
- null
- 0
- NaN (not a number)
- ''
- ""

The ones that are worth memorizing are 0, null, and an empty string. Let's hope you can remember that false is a falsy value.

Notice a few things conspicuously absent? If you wondered about the absence of arrays and objects (not to mention the other collection types), good eye. Arrays and objects, even empty arrays and objects, are always truthy. So you'll have to find another way to check emptiness with either [].length or Object.keys({}).length, which will give you either 0 or a nice truthy number.

Okay, you may be wondering why you should care about falsy values and truthy values (whatever is not falsy is truthy, of course). They're important because you can shorten a lot of otherwise lengthy expressions.

```
const employee = {
  name: 'Eric',
  equipmentTraining: '',
}
if(!employee.equipmentTraining) {
    return 'Not authorized to operate machinery';
}
```

You don't need the code to know anything about when they received their equipment training. The code doesn't need to know if it's a date or a certificate name. All that the code needs to know is that the value exists and there's something there.

---

1.   https://developer.mozilla.org/en-US/docs/Glossary/Falsy

But there are a few catches. Here's where things get tricky. It can be easy to create a falsy value unintentionally. The most common problem occurs when you're testing existence in an array by checking the index of a value:

```
['a', 'b'].indexOf('a')
// 0 which is falsy
```

You already saw this problem when you explored Array.includes(), so it should sneak up on you less often than it might have before. A much more subtle problem arises when you look for key-value data that's not defined. If you try to pull a value from a key that's not defined, you'll get undefined, which may cause a problem if an object or map were to change elsewhere in the code.

Let's change the object just a bit to make equipmentTraining a Boolean.

```
const employee = {
  name: 'Eric',
  equipmentTraining: true,
};
function listCerts(employee) {
    if(employee.equipmentTraining) {
        employee.certificates = ['Equipment'];

        // Mutation!
        delete employee.equipmentTraining;
    }
    // More code.
}
checkAuthorization() {
    if(!employee.equipmentTraining) {
        return 'Not authorized to operate machinery';
    }
    return 'Hello, ${employee.name}'
}
listCerts(employee);

checkAuthorization(employee);
// 'Not authorized to operate machinery'
```

What happened here? The function listCerts() mutated the object and removed the key-value data. In the next function, you tried to check a value on the object. On objects, if the key isn't defined, you don't get an error—you get undefined (the same is true for maps). This would be a puzzling bug because when you inspect the code, it looks like the employee has certifications and should pass the conditional. Once again, be very careful with mutations.

How can you solve the problem? There are actually two answers. Can you guess both of them?

The first, and far superior, solution is to not mutate the data. Falsy statements are way too valuable to give up. If a function is mutating the data, change the function.

If, for some reason, you're unable to do that, you can use a strict equivalency check to make sure the value is there and it's in the format you want. If you use strict equivalency, you can guard against a situation where someone sets employee.equipmentTraining to 'Not Trained', which is truthy.

```
checkAuthorization() {
    if(employee.equipmentTraining !== true) {
        return 'Not authorized to operate machinery';
    }
    return 'Hello, ${employee.name}'
}

checkAuthorization(employee);
// 'Not authorized to operate machinery'
```

More code, but that's okay. Things happen. You don't need to chain yourself to falsy values, but you should certainly understand them. They're about to play a big role.

In the next tip, you'll learn how to use falsy and truthy values to make quick data checks.

Tip 18

Check Data Quickly with the Ternary Operator

In this tip, you'll learn how to avoid reassignment with the ternary operator.

By now, you may have noticed that I love simple code. I'll always try to get an expression reduced down to the fewest characters I can. I blame a former coworker who reviewed some code I wrote at one of my first jobs.

```
if(active) {
    var display = 'bold'
} else {
    var display = 'normal'
}
```

He took one glance and casually said, "You should just make that a ternary."

"Of course," I agreed, not quite sure what he was talking about. After looking it up, I simplified the code to a one-line expression and my code has never been the same.

```
var display = active ? 'bold' : 'normal';
```

Chances are you've worked with ternary operators before. They're common in most languages, and they allow you to do a quick if/then check. (Although they aren't exclusively for this purpose, it is by far the most common usage.)

If the ternary operator isn't new, why should it interest you? In returning to some of the larger themes we've been exploring, ternary expressions allow your code to be not just more simple as I've mentioned, but also more predictable. They do this because they cut down on the number of variables that are being reassigned.

Besides, with new variable types, we hit some problems with excessive if/else statements. If you try to check a variable and you're using a block scoped variable, you won't be able to access the variable outside of the check.

```
conditionals/ternary/if.js
if (title === 'manager') {
  const permissions = ['time', 'pay'];
} else {
  const permissions = ['time'];
}
permissions;
// ReferenceError: permissions is not defined
```

Now you're forced to either use var, which is accessible outside the block scope, or you have to define the variable with let and then reassign it inside the if/else block. Here's how it would look with the assignment before the block:

conditionals/ternary/if.js
```
let permissions;
if (title === 'manager') {
  permissions = ['time', 'pay'];
} else {
  permissions = ['time'];
}
```

Before let and const, you didn't have to worry so much about when variables were created. Now, in addition to excessive code, there's a potential for scope conflicts.

Ternary expressions solve these problems. Clearly, they cut down on a lot of extra code. But they also allow you to be more predictable by assigning a value directly to const. How could you rewrite the preceding code to use const and a ternary?

conditionals/ternary/ternary.js
```
const permissions = title === 'manager' ? ['time', 'pay'] : ['time'];
```

Much cleaner *and* you now have a predictable value.

There's one caution you should keep in mind: Though you can chain multiple ternary expressions together, you should avoid doing so. Imagine that there's another user type called supervisor that couldn't see the pay rate but could authorize overtime. You might be tempted to just add another ternary expression. What's the harm, right?

conditionals/ternary/ternaryProblem.js
```
const permissions = title === 'supervisor' || title === 'manager' ?
  title === 'manager' ?
    ['time', 'overtimeAuthorization', 'pay'] : ['time', 'overtimeAuthorization']
  : ['time'];
```

At that point, the ternary becomes unreadable and loses the value of simplicity. Instead, you should move the check completely out of the block into a standalone function (with a nice test, of course). That way, you can still use const without worrying about excessive code.

conditionals/ternary/ternaryProblem.js
```
function getTimePermissions({ title }) {
  if (title === 'manager') {
    return ['time', 'overtimeAuthorization', 'pay'];
  }
```

```
  if (title === 'supervisor') {
    return ['time', 'overtimeAuthorization'];
  }
  return ['time'];
}
const permissions = getTimePermissions({ title: 'employee' });
// ['time']
```

There's no harm in making short functions that have a single non-abstract purpose. In fact, it's a good step to writing clean code. You still get the value of assigning the return value to const and everything is clear and readable. Ternary expressions can simplify things, but use them when they add value and go back to standard if blocks if they create too much ambiguity.

In the next tip, you'll make quick data checks even easier with short circuiting.

Tip 19

Maximize Efficiency with Short Circuiting

In this tip, you'll learn to reduce conditionals to the smallest possible expression with short circuiting.

You've been simplifying conditional expressions a lot in the last few tips. But there's one more level of simplification you can use: short circuiting.

As the name implies, the goal of short circuiting is to bypass information checks by placing the most relevant information first.

Consider the following ternary, which would fit in well with the discussion from the previous chapter.

```
conditionals/shortCircuiting/ternary.js
function getIconPath(icon) {
  const path = icon.path ? icon.path : 'uploads/default.png';
  return `https://assets.foo.com/${path}`;
}
```

The goal here is fairly clear. If an icon has a truthy path (in this case, that means it's defined and isn't an empty string), then you want to use the path. If it's falsy, undefined, or '', then you want to use the default.

```
const icon = {
    path: 'acme/bar.png'
}

getIconPath(icon);

// 'https://assets.foo.com/acme/bar.png';
```

Did you see any clues that suggest you can clean up this code a bit?

You probably noticed that you're writing the information check, icon.path, twice. Let's assume that data is always going to be valid, which means there's no difference between the information we're checking and the information we want. If it's truthy, we're going to use it.

Before updating the code, take a moment to think about how logical operators work. The or operator, symbolized as ||, will return true if any of the possible values are true. That means that as soon as one thing—anything—returns true, you don't care what the other values might be.

Now here's where it gets exciting. Because you can use truthy values to test a Boolean expression, true or false, there's no incentive for the language to change the value from something truthy to true. So if one value in an || check returns true, you get that truthy value and not true.

Lost? Don't worry. That's a long way of saying you can assign values directly from a Boolean check.

```
const name = 'joe' || 'I have no name';
name
// 'joe'
```

Now you have all of the tools you need to rewrite the ternary to something concise.

conditionals/shortCircuiting/shortCircuiting.js
```
function getIconPath(icon) {
  const path = icon.path || 'uploads/default.png';
  return `https://assets.foo.com/${path}`;
}
```

As you may have noticed, the best part is that you can append a default value to the end of the expression. This means that you never have to worry about a variable being falsy because you know there's a truthy value waiting at the end.

There you have it. You can use short circuiting to bypass information once something truthy occurs. How about the other way around? How can you halt an expression once something false occurs? That's possible as well.

Another popular usage of short circuiting is to prevent errors, particularly when you plan to use a method or action on a particular collection.

Consider a slight change to the problem of getting an icon. Instead of finding an icon set, you need to get a set of images from a user. The first image will be used as a thumbnail.

Because there are many images, the images collection will be an array. And your code needs to be able to handle the following representations:

```
// No array specified
const userConfig1 = {
}

// An array with no elements
const userConfig2 = {
    images: []
}
```

```
// An array with elements
const userConfig3 = {
    images: [
        'me.png',
        'work.png'
    ]
}
```

You may start off by thinking you could use short circuiting with the || operator to get the value you want. But that won't work for instances where the property isn't defined.

```
const userConfig1 = {
}

const img = userConfig1.images[0] || 'default.png';

//TypeError: Cannot read property '0' of undefined
```

The next step might be to use a series of nested conditionals.

conditionals/shortCircuiting/conditional.js

```
function getFirstImage(userConfig) {
  let img = 'default.png';
  if (userConfig.images) {
    img = userConfig.images[0];
  }
  return img;
}
```

At least in that example, you won't get an error if the images array isn't defined. But it will create a problem if there are no elements of the array.

```
const userConfig = {
    images: []
}

const img = getFirstImage(userConfig);

//undefined
```

Now to solve that problem, you might add another nested conditional.

conditionals/shortCircuiting/conditional.js

```
function getImage(userConfig) {
  let img = 'default.png';
  if (userConfig.images) {
    if (userConfig.images.length) {
      img = userConfig.images[0];
    }
  }
  return img;
}
```

Things are already starting to get a little ugly and unreadable.

Fortunately, short circuiting can help. Combining conditionals with the && operator will allow you to avoid the TypeError you saw earlier. A logical string built with an && operator will cease as soon as a false value occurs. This means that you don't have worry about a TypeError when you try to call a method that doesn't exist. You can safely check for the existence of a collection and then call a method on it.

```
conditionals/shortCircuiting/shortCircuiting.js
function getImage(userConfig) {
  if (userConfig.images && userConfig.images.length > 0) {
    return userConfig.images[0];
  }
  return 'default.png';
}
```

Now, this isn't perfect because you're just checking for a truthy value, which means that if there's bad data and images is set to a string, you'll get a weird result (the first letter of the string). But I'd leave it the way it is. At some point, you have to have a little trust in your data or you need to find a way to normalize the data higher up the stream.

Finally, you can combine your short circuiting back with a ternary to get this check down to a one liner. Start by pulling the images property into its own variable. Remember that if it's not there, the variable will merely be undefined.

```
conditionals/shortCircuiting/ternary.js
function getImage(userConfig) {
  const images = userConfig.images;
  return images && images.length ? images[0] : 'default.png';
}
```

Be careful when combining ternaries and short circuiting. Things can get out of hand very quickly. Say, for example, that you want to make sure the image didn't have a GIF extension. You'd still have to make sure there are elements in the array, or else you'd get another TypeError by checking for an index value on undefined. The resulting code is getting crazy.

```
conditionals/shortCircuiting/ternary.js
const images = userConfig.images;
return images &&
          images.length &&
          images[0].indexOf('gif') < 0
  ? images[0] : 'default.png';
```

You could refactor your code to check for an image. Or you could check the extension with a regular expression instead of an index. There are lots of ways around the problem. At some point, you need to make sure your conditionals are making code more clear and not just shorter for the sake of being short.

There's no explicit rule about how many conditionals are too many. It's more a matter of taste and team agreement. But when things get long (usually around three conditional checks), it's better to make it a standalone function.

Simplicity is great. And it's fun to try and find clever ways to reduce things to one line. But the goal is always communication and readability. Use short circuiting to make things readable—not to make code artificially small.

Now that you can make simple conditionals, it's time to put that knowledge into action.

In the next chapter, you'll explore loops and how you can create simplified loops that avoid mutations, return predictable results, and can be as short as a single line of code.

CHAPTER 5

Simplify Loops

My auto mechanics teacher in high school once started off class by holding up a large adjustable wrench. "Some people think this is the only tool they need," he said. He demonstrated how someone could use the wrench to unscrew a bolt, take off a screw, and pry off a gasket like a set of pliers. "They even use it as a hammer," he said as he swung the wrench in the air.

"But if all you use is a wrench, you'll round off your bolts. You'll snap off fan blades, dent your car, and generally make things worse." As he finished, he placed the wrench on the bench. "And that's why we have specialized tools," he said as he showed us how to use ratchet wrenches, torque wrenches, spark plug gap gauges, and all the other tools a good mechanic keeps at hand.

You're about to get your specialized set of tools for looping through data in JavaScript. When you use the right tool, your code will be more clear, and you'll signal your intentions to other developers.

You've almost certainly used a for loop before. If you wanted to convert an array of integers to strings, you could easily use a for loop. You simply need to create an empty array, loop through the values one at a time using the index from the for loop, and push the new values into new array.

But you know that will just create problems. You'll have more variables to keep track of. You'll have mutations. And other developers will have no clue what you're trying to accomplish. When you use one type of loop, other developers won't know if you're returning all results of an original array or just a subset. They won't know at a glance if you're converting data types or changing the collection from an array to an object.

If you try to solve every problem with one tool, your code will be complex and hard to use. You need better tools.

We're going to start off by jumping ahead a bit to see how to use arrow functions. Arrow functions turn simple loops into one-liners. Next, you'll get an in-depth look at how array methods simplify loops and how you can know what to expect based on the specialized loop. From there, we'll explore several different array methods one at a time. We'll start with map(), which pulls the same information out from each collection. We'll look at a series of specialized loops that do one task well, finishing with the most flexible loop, reduce(), which can do pretty much anything. We'll wrap up by exploring the updated for...of and for...in loops, which use clear variable names instead of indexes.

The best mechanics can always grab the right tool for the job. Coding is no different. If you look at the best code, you'll notice the developers always use the loop that fits their intentions. These new loops take practice and can be confusing. But before you know it, you'll be able to use them with ease, and you'll love how clear and expressive you've made your code. Special tools exist for a reason. Time to learn how to use them. To start, take a look at one of the most beloved new features in JavaScript: arrow functions.

Tip 20

Simplify Looping with Arrow Functions

In this tip, you'll learn to cut out extraneous information with arrow functions.

In JavaScript, you see a lot of callback functions. Those are functions that are passed as a parameter to other functions. Most of the loops you're about to learn depend on callbacks.

Like most pre-ES6 code, functions are wordy. You have to explicitly declare that you're creating a function with the function keyword, add curly braces to signify the body, use return statements to end the function, and so on. It's not unusual for the callback to be longer than the function you inject it into.

Arrow functions changed that and made writing functions simple and short. And learning about them now will make all the loops you see in future tips much more interesting. It will come as no surprise that arrow functions combined with array methods have led some to abandon for loops altogether.

Well then, what are arrow functions? Arrow functions strip away as much extraneous information as possible.

How much extraneous information is there in a function? Quite a bit. It turns out, you can communicate a function without:

- The word function
- Parentheses around arguments
- The word return
- Curly braces

All you need to do is use the fat arrow => to indicate that you'll be building a function. You might be thinking that you've just lost everything that makes a function a function. It's true you can get functions to a minimal state, but there are still a few rules you must follow.

Before you begin, you should know that arrow functions look simple, but they actually have a lot of subtle quirks. Fortunately, you don't need to understand subtleties now. You'll get to those when you explore them more in Tip 36, *Prevent Context Confusion with Arrow Functions*, on page 171. To start, look at a function that still has most of the extra stuff (parentheses, curly braces, return statements).

Here's a simple function that takes an argument and returns a slightly modified value. In this case, it takes a name and returns the name with a capitalized first letter.

loops/arrow/full.js
```
function capitalize(name) {
  return name[0].toUpperCase() + name.slice(1);
}
```

Easy, right? But before you can translate this into an arrow function, you should notice that this is a named function. All that means is the name is declared as part of a function, like this:

```
function namedFunction() {

}
```

That's not the only way to create a function. You can also create an anonymous function—a function that doesn't have a name—and assign it to a variable:

```
const assignedFunction = function() {

}
```

Here's the same function as an anonymous function. Everything is the same except you're assigning it to a variable.

loops/arrow/anonymous.js
```
const capitalize = function (name) {
  return name[0].toUpperCase() + name.slice(1);
};
```

An arrow function version uses the same idea: an anonymous function you assign to a variable. You can remove the function keyword and replace it with a fat arrow. As a bonus, if you have exactly one parameter (which will be the case for many array methods), you can dispense with the parentheses.

loops/arrow/arrow.js
```
const capitalize = name => {
  return name[0].toUpperCase() + name.slice(1);
};
```

That's all there is to it. You'll dive deep into where and how to use arrow functions later. For now, look at how normal functions translate to regular functions. To keep it quick, you'll get a rule, then a named function version, then an arrow version. But please try and write it out before you look at the translation. This feature is supported right now in many browsers, so open up a Chrome console and try it out.

That last example took one parameter, which means that you don't need the parameters. But if you have no parameters, you still need parentheses.

Before:

loops/arrow/full.js
```
function key() {
  return 'abc123';
}
```

After:

loops/arrow/arrow.js
```
const key = () => {
  return 'abc123';
};
```

If you have more than one parameter, you'll also need to use parentheses

Before:

loops/arrow/full.js
```
function greet(first, last) {
  return `Oh, hi ${capitalize(first)} ${capitalize(last)}`;
}
```

After:

loops/arrow/arrow.js
```
const greet = (first, last) => {
  return `Oh, hi ${capitalize(first)} ${capitalize(last)}`;
};
```

When the body of your function (the part normally inside the curly braces) is only one line, you can move everything—the fat arrow, the parameters, the return statement—to a single line.

And if the function itself is only one line, you don't even need to use the return keyword. In other words, you return the result of the function body line automatically.

Before:

loops/arrow/full.js
```
function formatUser(name) {
  return `${capitalize(name)} is logged in.`;
}
```

After:

loops/arrow/arrow.js
```
const formatUser = name => `${capitalize(name)} is logged in.`;
```

Finally, you can use arrow functions as anonymous functions without needing to assign them to variables. This is how you'll be using it the most in the upcoming tips, so it's worth a look on its own.

In JavaScript, you can pass a function as an argument to another function. Functions are just another form of data. Passing a function as an argument is very common for functions that take a callback, a function that will be executed at the end of the logic of the original function.

Here you have a simple function that will apply a custom greeting. You're passing in a function to return a custom greeting as a callback. This is sometimes called injecting a function.

loops/arrow/full.js
```
function applyCustomGreeting(name, callback) {
  return callback(capitalize(name));
}
```

It's perfectly okay to create a named function and pass that in. But often, it's just more convenient to create an anonymous function when you call the original function. In other words, you can call the function applyCustomGreeting() and pass in an anonymous function that you write on the spot. You never assign it to a variable first.

loops/arrow/full.js
```
applyCustomGreeting('mark', function (name) {
  return `Oh, hi ${name}!`;
});
```

What do you have here? You have a simple anonymous function that takes a single parameter with a body that's a single line long, and that single line is just a return statement. This is exactly the situation where arrow functions excel. That anonymous function has so much of that extra fluff you don't need.

Now that you have the tools, try rewriting the anonymous function as an arrow function. You'll get something like this:

loops/arrow/arrow.js
```
applyCustomGreeting('mark', name => `Oh, hi ${name}!`);
```

I hope you like the look of that because you're about to see a lot more of that kind of function as you work through array methods. Array methods and arrow functions are convenient ways to update a collection of data.

In the next tip, you'll learn why array methods prevent a lot of mutations and extraneous variables. You'll start to see why they've become so popular in JavaScript.

Tip 21

Write Shorter Loops with Array Methods

In this tip, you'll learn to reduce long loops to single lines with array methods.

Before we begin, I want you to know that for loops and for...of loops are good. You'll want to use them, and you should use them. They're never going away.

But you should use them less. Why? Well, the reason is simple: They're unnecessary clutter. You're writing modern JavaScript, which means you're going for simplicity, readability, and predictability, and traditional loops don't meet those goals. Array methods do. Mastering array methods is the fastest way to improve your JavaScript code.

Look at this basic loop that converts an array of price strings into floating point values.

loops/methods/problem.js
```
const prices = ['1.0', '2.15'];

const formattedPrices = [];
for (let i = 0; i < prices.length; i++) {
  formattedPrices.push(parseFloat(prices[i]));
}
```

It's short, sure. The whole thing takes four lines. Not bad. But consider a file that has five functions. And each function has a loop. You just added 20 lines to the file.

And this function is pretty short to begin with. What if you had an array that contained some non-numerical strings and you wanted only parsable numbers? Your function starts to grow.

loops/methods/problem.js
```
Line 1  const prices = ['1.0', 'negotiable', '2.15'];
     2
     3  const formattedPrices = [];
     4  for (let i = 0; i < prices.length; i++) {
     5    const price = parseFloat(prices[i]);
     6    if (price) {
     7      formattedPrices.push(price);
     8    }
     9  }
```

Clutter. Clutter. Clutter. Just look at all the extra stuff you need just to get the float prices. On line 3, you declare a new collection before you even begin working with the data. And before you even enter the for loop, you're facing a paradox. Because let is block scoped, you have to declare the collection outside of the loop. Now you have an extraneous array with no members sitting outside the loop.

Next, you have to follow the crazy three-part pattern to declare the iterator on line 4. You can often get around that with a for...of loop, but many times, you still need to declare the iterator.

And finally, you're mixing two different concerns: transforming the value and filtering out bad values with your conditional on line 6. This isn't a horrible problem, but it does hurt predictability. Is the code standardizing the values in the array or is it filtering out unwanted values? In this case, it does both.

Is it simple? No. It takes multiple lines and several variable declarations.

Is it readable? Sure. But as the number of lines grows, the file decreases in readability.

Is it predictable? No. It creates an empty array that may or may not be changed later because it's not a constant (and yes, you can push to a variable defined with const, but that's a no-no). Besides, we can't predict at a glance if formattedPrices will include everything. In this case, it won't. In the first case, it will. There's no clue inherent in the action.

Array methods are a great way to get clean predictable code with no extraneous data. Some find them intimidating, but with a little effort, you'll master them quickly and find your code better than ever.

The most popular array methods change either the size array or the shape of the data in the array. There's one big exception: the reduce() method. But you'll get to that soon enough.

What does size and shape even mean? Look at a simple array of members of a digital marketing team.

```
const team = [
    {
        name: 'melinda',
        position: 'ux designer'
    },
    {
        name: 'katie',
        position: 'strategist'
    },
```

```
    {
        name: 'madhavi',
        position: 'developer'
    },
    {
        name: 'justin',
        position: 'manager'
    },
    {
        name: 'chris',
        position: 'developer'
    }
]
```

At a glance, you can clearly see that this array has a size of five objects. You can also see that every item has a shape: a name and a position.

Nearly any array method you choose will alter either the size or the shape of the return array. You simply need to decide if you want to change the size or the shape (or both).

Do you want to change the size by reducing the number of members in the array by removing them? Do you want to change the shape by only getting the names of the team members? Do you want to do both and get the names of just the developers?

You'll explore all these in upcoming tips, but here's a cheat sheet:

- map()
  - Action: Changes the shape, but not the size.
  - Example: Get the name of everyone on the team.
  - Result: ['melinda', 'katie', 'madhavi', 'justin', 'chris']

- sort()
  - Action: Changes neither the size nor the shape, but changes the order.
  - Example: Get the team members in alphabetical order.
  - Result: [{name: 'chris', position: 'developer'}, {name: 'justin' ...}]

- filter()
  - Action: Changes the size, but not the shape.
  - Example: Get the developers.
  - Result: [{name: 'madhavi', position: 'developer'}, {name: 'chris', position:'developer'}]

- find()
  - Action: Changes the size to exactly one, but not the shape. Does *not* return an array.

- Example: Get the manager.
- Result: {name: 'justin', position: 'manager'}

- forEach()
  - Action: Uses the shape, but returns nothing.
  - Example: Give all members a bonus!
  - Result: Melinda gets a bonus! Katie get a bonus!... (but no return value).

- reduce()
  - Action: Changes the size and the shape to pretty much anything you want.
  - Example: Get the total developers and non-developers.
  - Result: {developers: 2, non-developers: 3}

Now that you can see all the options ahead, I'm sure you're excited to get started. Well, you don't have to wait any longer! Here's how you can rewrite the for loop using an array method.

loops/methods/methods.js
```
const prices = ['1.0', '2.15'];
const formattedPrices = prices.map(price => parseFloat(price));
// [1.0, 2.15];
```

Try evaluating the code using the usual criteria: simple, readable, predictable.

Is it simple? Yes. Everything fits on a single line.

Is it readable? Yes. You can see the action on one line. As the file grows, the number of lines won't grow any faster than the number of simple actions.

Is it predictable? Yes. The value is assigned with const so you know it won't change. And because you used a map, you know that you'll have an array of exactly the same size. At a glance, you can tell that the goal is to get the float values with parseFloat(). So you also know that the array will be the exact size as the original with only float values.

I know what you're going to say: You may have solved the simple loop, but what about the more complicated loop that removes false values?

Fortunately, array methods can be chained. That means you can call one right after the other and it will pass the result down to the next item.

loops/methods/methods.js
```
const prices = ['1.0', 'negotiable', '2.15'];
const formattedPrices = prices.map(price => parseFloat(price))
// [1.0, NaN, 2.15]
  .filter(price => price);
// [1.0, 2.15]
```

First you convert values to floating point while keeping the array the same size. Then you change the size, but not shape, by pulling out false values.

The process is much easier to follow, and because you can chain them together, you can still assign the resulting array with const.

Do I have your interest now? Awesome. Because it's time to dive into writing your own array methods. You'll find you'll use the same methods over and over. But remember—they each have their strengths. If you become frustrated trying to fit an action into a method, try using a different method or think about how you can break the action into pieces and chain it together.

Now that you have the foundation, it's time to jump in. In the next tip, you'll start changing the shape of members of an array with map().

| Tip 22 |

Create Arrays of a Similar Size with map()

In this tip, you'll learn how to pull out a subset of information from an array using map().

In the previous tip, you saw how you could rewrite a simple for loop with an array method. Now you're going to start exploring how to use specific array methods.

You'll begin with map() (not to be confused with the Map object). It's fairly common, and your new array receives the information you return in a brand new array. In other words, the return value is transparent, which isn't the case with other array methods. Here's another good reason to start with map(): the name "map" isn't very expressive. What does that even mean? When I first learned it, I needed a fair amount of experience before I could see and understand a map function at a glance.

Your goal is to get an idea of how most array methods work. And your secondary goal is to gain enough experience with map() that you'll start to see why it's one of the most popular methods.

Start with a simple map function. A map function takes a piece of information from an input array and returns something new. Sometimes it returns part of the information. Other times, it transforms the information and returns the new value. That means it can take a single property from an array, or it can take a value in an array and return an altered version. For example, it can return an array with all the values capitalized or converted from integers to currency.

The easiest example is pulling specific information from an object. Let's start with a collection of musicians.

loops/map/map.js
```
const band = [
  {
    name: 'corbett',
    instrument: 'guitar',
  },
  {
    name: 'evan',
    instrument: 'guitar',
  },
```

```
  {
    name: 'sean',
    instrument: 'bass',
  },
  {
    name: 'brett',
    instrument: 'drums',
  },
];
```

You have the band, but what you really want is just a list of instruments the band members play.

Every array method takes a callback function that you'll apply to each member of the array. These functions are very simple by design. They can only take one argument: the individual member of an array (the reduce() method is an exception that we'll discuss later).

Before you dive into building a map function, create a basic for loop to use as a comparison. Once you have that loop, you'll start slowly refactoring it until you get to a working map function. This will help you gain an understanding for how a map() function is just a simplified loop.

Okay, here's a simple for loop to get the band instruments:

loops/map/full.js
```
Line 1  const instruments = [];
     2  for (let i = 0; i < band.length; i++) {
     3    const instrument = band[i].instrument;
     4    instruments.push(instrument);
     5  }
```

Now it's time to start refactoring. The first thing to do is to combine line 3 and line 4. Instead of getting the instrument and passing it to the push method, you'll get the instrument as part of the argument for push(). To keep things readable, put the logic to retrieve the instrument into a separate function.

You'll get a function that looks like this:

loops/map/full.js
```
function getInstrument(member) {
  return member.instrument;
}
```

Sure it doesn't shorten things up much, but it helps. And more important, you've made a huge step by separating the iterator band[i] and the information you want from the individual member: member.instrument. Remember that with map() methods, you want to think about the individual pieces, not the whole array.

Here's how your new method fits into the current for loop:

```
loops/map/full.js
const instruments = [];
for (let i = 0; i < band.length; i++) {
  instruments.push(getInstrument(band[i]));
}
```

At this point, you've pretty much written your map function.

With map(), there's no need to set up a return array—that's included as part of the array method. There's also no need to push information. map() pushes the result of the function into its own return array.

The only thing you need for map() is a function that takes each item as an argument and returns something to put in the return array. What do you know—you already have that written out!

Most of the time, you'll just write an anonymous function for an array method, but that's not a requirement. You can name a function if you want (and sometimes that's a smart move for testing purposes). That means you can reuse the getInstrument() function you already have and pass it directly to map(). At this point, you can abandon your for loop.

```
loops/map/map.js
function getInstrument(member) {
  return member.instrument;
}

const instruments = band.map(getInstrument);
// ['guitar', 'guitar', 'bass', 'drums']
```

Look at what you've accomplished. You removed excess code while keeping things more transparent:

- You *know* you're going to get an array. You don't need to define one ahead of time.

- You *know* it will be the same size as the original array.

- You *know* it will contain the instruments and nothing else.

Predictable and simple.

If you understand this, congratulations—you understand most array methods. All array methods are just methods that take a callback that act on each member of an array. The type of array method determines what happens with the return value of that function. But writing the function itself is very similar for each array method.

Now that you've refactored your for loop to a map method, you can take the next step and convert the named function to an anonymous function. Remember those arrow functions you just learned? Now is a perfect time to use them.

You're taking a single argument, so you don't need parentheses. And the body of the function is only one line long, so you don't need curly braces or a return statement. Go ahead and try writing it out. These functions become much easier with practice.

```
loops/map/map.js
const instruments = band.map(member => member.instrument);
// ['guitar', 'guitar', 'bass', 'drums']
```

map() is fairly simple, but it's flexible. You can use it for anything—yes, any-thing—when the goal is to have an array of the same size. Up to now, you've only been elevating data from an array of objects. But you can also transform information, as you saw when you converted strings to values with parseInt() in the previous tip.

In the next tip, you'll see an array method that does something a little different. You'll maintain the shape of the array items, but you'll return only a subset by performing a true or false check on each item.

Tip 23

Pull Out Subsets of Data with filter() and find()

In this tip, you'll learn how to change the size of an array while retaining the shape of the items.

In the previous tip, you created a new array by pulling out only the relevant information from the original array. You'll likely encounter situations where you want to keep the shape of the data, but you only want a subset of the total items. Maybe you only want users that live in a certain city, but you still need all their information. The array method filter() will perform this exact action. Unlike the map() method, you aren't changing any information in the array—you're just reducing what you get back.

As an example, let's filter a simple array of strings. You have a team of people, and you want only people named some form of Dave (David, Davis, Davina, and so on). In my hometown, there's a sandwich shop that gives out a free sandwich once a year to anyone named Joe/Joseph/Joanna, so being able to filter people by name variant is a crucial task. You wouldn't want to deprive your Daves or Joes of a delicious lunch.

Start with a list of coworkers that you want to reduce down.

```
loops/filter/full.js
const team = [
  'Michelle B',
  'Dave L',
  'Dave C',
  'Courtney B',
  'Davina M',
];
```

You'll need to check to see if the string contains a form of "Dav" using the match() method on a string. This method will return an array of information if the string matches a regular expression matches and null if there's no match. In other words, match() will return a truthy value, an array, if there's a regex match and a falsy value, null, if there is none.

```
'Dave'.match(/Dav/);
// ['Dav', index: 0, input: 'Dave']

'Michelle'.match(/Dav/);
// null
```

Traditionally, you'd solve the problem with a for loop. And as you've probably guessed by now, the solution isn't pretty.

```
loops/filter/full.js
const daves = [];
for (let i = 0; i < team.length; i++) {
  if (team[i].match(/Dav/)) {
    daves.push(team[i]);
  }
}
```

A filter function can do the exact same thing in a single line. Like the map() method, you call the method on an array and you get an array back.

There's one trick. Unlike the map() method, the function you pass into the filter() method must return a truthy value. When you iterate over each item, if it returns something truthy, it's retained. If it doesn't return a truthy value, it isn't retained. See why it's important to have a solid grasp of truthiness (the programmer kind, not the Colbert kind). Say you want to get the passing scores from an array. The filter function would take each score and say whether it was above the threshold (60) and keeps it if it is.

```
loops/filter/filter.js
const scores = [30, 82, 70, 45];
function getNumberOfPassingScores(scores) {
  const passing = scores.filter(score => score > 59);
  // [70, 82]
  return passing.length;
}
// 2
```

The function returns either true or false, but the final array contains the actual values of 82 and 70. The function checked each score one at a time, retaining the score (not the return value) if the return value was true. Note also, the return array preserves the order of the original.

Most important, filter() will always return an array, even if nothing matches the values. If you wanted to see how many perfect scores you'd get, you may be a little disappointed. But you can still confidently call the length property knowing you'll have an array of some sort. Simple and predictable.

```
loops/filter/filter.js
function getPerfectScores(scores) {
  const perfect = scores.filter(score => score === 100);
  // []
  return perfect.length;
}
// 0
```

To return to your hungry Daves: In the previous anonymous functions you pass to filter(), you're returning a Boolean—true or false—while in this one, you want to check a string. Because match() returns truthy and falsy values, you can use it directly in the filter function.

Here's your simplified loop:

loops/filter/filter.js
```
const daves = team.filter(member => member.match(/Dav/));
```

Filter is so easy to use that there's not much left to say. Still, there's one variation that can be very useful.

On occasion, you might be lucky enough to know that there will be at most one match (or you're only interested in one match) in your array. In that case, you can use a method that's similar to filter() called find(). The find() method takes a function as argument, a function that returns a truthy or falsy value, and returns only the first result that evaluates to true. If there's no true value, it returns undefined.

This is great when you know there will only be one value—looking for an entry with a specific ID, for example. Or if you want the first instance of a particular item—getting the last update to a page by a particular user on a sorted array.

Here's a good way to think about this: If you'd normally use a break statement in a loop, the action is a good candidate for find().

Let's say you're writing a scheduling app for library instructors. Each instructor works in several locations, but no location has more than one instructor.

Your array of instructors would look like this:

loops/filter/full.js
```
const instructors = [
  {
    name: 'Jim',
    libraries: ['MERIT'],
  },
  {
    name: 'Sarah',
    libraries: ['Memorial', 'SLIS'],
  },
  {
    name: 'Eliot',
    libraries: ['College Library'],
  },
];
```

If you were to write a for loop to check it, you'd go through each one and break when you get to the correct result.

```
loops/filter/full.js
let memorialInstructor;
for (let i = 0; i < instructors.length; i++) {
  if (instructors[i].libraries.includes('Memorial')) {
    memorialInstructor = instructors[i];
    break;
  }
}
```

This loop will check the first instructor and see that he doesn't meet the criteria. The second instructor does meet the criteria, saving the incredible labor of looking at the third instructor. Of course, in real-world data, there may be hundreds or even thousands of results. Stopping at the first instance is a nice little optimization to avoid iterating over the whole set.

How does this translate into a find() function? It's simple: The if block contains everything you need to change this into a find() function. Using the ideas from filter(), try to write it out.

You probably came up with something like this:

```
loops/filter/filter.js
const librarian = instructors.find(instructor => {
  return instructor.libraries.includes('Memorial');
});
```

Once again, you've reduced several lines down to a simple expression (could be a one-liner, but it runs off the printed page!) while simultaneously removing an unstable let with a predictable const. The only down-side to using find() is that you can't be absolutely sure of the return value. If there's no match, you get undefined, while with filter() you'd get an empty array if there were no matches. But using your knowledge of short circuiting, you can always add an or statement combined with a default.

```
const image = [
    {
        path: './me.jpg',
        profile:false
    }
];
const profile = images.find(image => image.profile) || {path:
'./default.jpg'};
```

There may be one thing bothering you about that find() function: You had to hard code the name of the library, Memorial. The challenge with an array function is that it takes a single argument, the item being checked. This is a problem if you want to add a second parameter, a variable to check the item against.

What do you do if you want to check against another location? Fortunately, you don't need to write a function for every library. Rather, you'd use a technique called currying to reduce the number of arguments down to one. You'll see this a lot more in Tip 34, *Maintain Single Responsibility Parameters with Partially Applied Functions*, on page 160, but it's one of my favorite techniques, so I'll go ahead and give you a taste.

loops/filter/filter.js
```
const findByLibrary = library => instructor => {
  return instructor.libraries.includes(library);
};
const librarian = instructors.find(findByLibrary('MERIT'));

// {
//   name: 'Jim',
//   libraries: ['MERIT'],
// }
```

But don't get too far ahead. There are more array methods to explore.

In the next tip, you'll break the pattern of returning a new array by using forEach() to perform an action on each array without getting any return values.

Tip 24

Apply Consistent Actions with forEach()

In this tip, you'll learn how to apply an action to each member of an array with forEach().

Things are going to get a little different in this tip. The two array methods you've explored so far return a new, altered array. You either changed the shape by pulling out a subset of information on each item, or you changed the size by returning only part of the total number of items.

In this tip, you aren't changing the input array at all. Instead, you're going to perform an action on every member. This is common when you finally get an array to the size and shape you want and then you want to do something with that data.

As an example, say you have a club with a group of members and you want to write a script to send an invitation to every club member when the next meeting is scheduled. You want a function that takes each member individually so that you can use other information—name, email, and so on—to customize the message.

Here's a list of members:

loops/forEach/forEach.js
```
const sailingClub = [
  'yi hong',
  'andy',
  'darcy',
  'jessi',
  'alex',
  'nathan',
];
```

Don't worry about the implementation details of the email function. All you need to know is that it takes a member object. As always, you could easily achieve your goal with a simple for loop.

loops/forEach/full.js
```
for (let i = 0; i < sailingClub.length; i++) {
  sendEmail(sailingClub[i]);
}
```

You really can't get much simpler than that. Unlike other methods, forEach() isn't valuable because it makes your code simpler. It's valuable because it's predictable and because it works like other array methods so it can be chained together (you'll see more about that in the next tip) with other methods.

The forEach() method, like all you've seen before, takes a function that takes a single argument: the individual member of the array. Unlike the other methods, the return statement (whether explicitly or implicitly defined) does absolutely nothing. Any action you take must affect something outside the function. Changing something outside the scope of the function is called a side effect, and though it's not horrible, it should be exercised with caution.

In other words, if you use forEach() to transform some names to uppercase, you'd get no results. This method does nothing unless you have a side effect of some sort. (By the way, this is why you should always test your code.) This code would effectively do nothing:

loops/forEach/forEach.js
```
const names = ['walter', 'white'];
const capitalized = names.forEach(name => name.toUpperCase());

capitalized;
// undefined
```

You could have a container array to collect the change result, but by now, you know that's bad because it mutates the capitalized array. Besides, that isn't even necessary because map() does the same thing.

loops/forEach/forEach.js
```
const names = ['walter', 'white'];
let capitalized = [];
names.forEach(name => capitalized.push(name.toUpperCase()));

capitalized;
// ['WALTER', 'WHITE'];
```

So when should you use forEach()? The best time is precisely when you want to perform an action outside the scope of the function. In other words, when you know you must cause a side effect, you should use forEach().

As it happens, that's exactly what you're doing when you send an invitation. You're causing a side effect—sending an email—but you aren't mutating any data (you assume).

Here's the updated action:

loops/forEach/forEach.js
```
sailingClub.forEach(member => sendEmail(member));
```

Three lines down to one line isn't bad, but it's certainly no cause for celebration.

So what's the point? The point is that you do get some predictability. When you see a forEach(), you know there's going to be a side effect. And as you learned in Tip 1, *Signal Unchanging Values with const*, on page 3, if you can't be certain of something, the next best option is knowing that there *might* be instability.

Even with that, the best reason to keep forEach() in your toolbox is that you can combine it with other array methods in a process called chaining. That means that you can perform multiple actions on the same array without needing to save the output to variables each time.

In the next tip, you'll use chaining to combine several actions into one process.

Tip 25

Combine Methods with Chaining

In this tip, you'll learn to perform multiple array methods with chaining.

Chaining is an old concept in programming. You can find it in many object-oriented languages.[1] Like a lot of programming concepts, it actually sounds more complicated than it is in practice.

Here's a quick definition: Chaining is immediately calling a method on a returned object (which in some cases is the original object) without reassigning the value first.

Okay, now forget that definition. For our purposes, chaining means that you can call several array methods in a row (as long as you get an array back). It's a convenient way to perform several actions in a very clear manner.

Think back to the last example: sending notifications to club members. The example was simplified (as examples always are). An actual array of club members would have a lot more data. It would have member status, email addresses, mailing addresses, position, and so on.

To keep things simple, let's add just two fields: active and email.

```
loops/chain/chain.js
const sailors = [
  {
    name: 'yi hong',
    active: true,
    email: 'yh@yhproductions.io',
  },
  {
    name: 'alex',
    active: true,
    email: '',
  },
  {
    name: 'nathan',
    active: false,
    email: '',
  },
];
```

---

1. https://en.wikipedia.org/wiki/Method_chaining

There's not much more information, but you have enough that you can be more sophisticated about whom you email. First, you can filter out all the inactive members—they won't want an invitation.

loops/chain/full.js
```
const active = sailors.filter(sailor => sailor.active);

// [
//   {
//     name: 'yi hong',
//     active: true,
//     email: 'yh@yhproductions.io',
//   },
//   {
//     name: 'alex',
//     active: true,
//     email: '',
//   },
// ];
```

Next, you can normalize the email addresses. If members have an email set, use that. Otherwise, use their default club email address.

loops/chain/full.js
```
const emails = active.map(member => member.email
              || `${member.name}@wiscsail.io`);

// [ 'yh@yhproductions.io', 'alex@wiscsail.io' ]
```

Finally, after the inactive members are removed and the email addresses are normalized, you can call sendInvitation() with the correct member information.

loops/chain/full.js
```
emails.forEach(sailor => sendEmail(sailor));
```

Notice that you assigned the result to a variable each time. With chaining, that's not necessary. Instead, you can remove the intermediate step of assigning to a variable by calling a method directly on the result.

Because filter() always returns an array (even if it's an empty array), you know that you can call any other array method on it. Similarly, because map() *always* returns an array, you can call another array method on it. Crucially, though, the final method—forEach()—doesn't return an array, so you can't call another method. In fact, it returns nothing, so you can't even assign the output of the whole group of actions to a variable.

Removing the intermediate steps, you get an identical set of actions without any variable declarations.

loops/chain/chain.js
```
sailors
  .filter(sailor => sailor.active)
  .map(sailor => sailor.email || `${sailor.name}@wiscsail.io`)
  .forEach(sailor => sendEmail(sailor));
```

Now you're sending an email to the preferred email address of only active members. The best part is that because each array method does one very specific thing, you can understand the code at a glance.

The only downside to chaining array methods is that each time you call a new method, you're iterating over the whole returned array. Instead of three iterations—one for each member—if you performed all actions with a for loop, you're performing seven iterations (three on the original array plus two more when mapping plus two more when calling forEach()). Don't pay too much attention to this. It's not terribly important unless you're working with large data sets. Sometimes the minor performance increase is worth extra readability. Sometimes it's not. It's just something to keep in mind.

There are a few tricks to chaining methods: First, notice how there are no semicolons until the final statement. The whole action is like a sentence. It's not over until you hit the period, even when it spans multiple lines.

This is one reason that many style guides still prefer semicolons even though they aren't strictly necessary in JavaScript. If you mess up and include a semicolon earlier, you'll get a SyntaxError so it's unlikely you'll get too far with that mistake.

More important, order does matter. You couldn't, for example, flip the filter() and the map() methods because the map() method would remove the property the filter() method would need to check. With this example at least, that would be very bad. You wouldn't get an error because sailor.active would return undefined for everything. The resulting array would be empty, which isn't an error. In other words, syntactically, everything makes sense even if you provide an empty array to forEach().

This is why it always pays to have a test. Check out the test suite for this book to see examples.[2]

Chaining isn't limited to array methods, but because arrays have so many methods that return arrays, they're very convenient examples to explore. You'll see more chaining as you continue. It pops up again and again. You may remember seeing using it with the Map object in Tip 13, *Update Key-Value*

Data Clearly with Maps, on page 54 when you chained multiple set() methods. And you'll see it again when you work with promises in Tip 43, *Retrieve Data Asynchronously with Promises*, on page 205. It's a simple but important concept that's worth reviewing several times.

In the next tip, you'll go back and look at one more array method, reduce(). It's the most flexible and interesting, but it's also the most unpredictable.

Tip 26

Transform Array Data with reduce()

In this tip, you'll learn how use reduce() to generate a new array with a different size and shape.

You're probably tired of hearing me say that good code is predictable. But it's true. Array methods are wonderful because you have an idea of the result at a glance without even understanding the callback function. Not only that, but array methods are easier to test and, as you'll see in Tip 32, *Write Functions for Testability*, on page 151, it's much easier to write testable code than it is to add tests to complex code.

Still, there are times when you need to create a new, radically different piece of data from an array. Maybe you need to get a count of certain items. Maybe you want to transform the array to a different structure, such as an object. That's where reduce() comes in. The reduce() method is different from other array methods in several ways, but the most important is that it can change both the size and the shape of data (or just one or just the other). And it doesn't necessarily return an array.

As usual, it's much easier to see than to explain. Here's a reduce function that returns the exact same array. It's useless, but it lets you see how a reduce() function is built.

loops/reduce/reduce.js
```
Line 1  const callback = function (collectedValues, item) {
     2    return [...collectedValues, item];
     3  };
     4
     5  const saying = ['veni', 'vedi', 'veci'];
     6  const initialValue = [];
     7  const copy = saying.reduce(callback, initialValue);
```

What's going on here? To start, notice that you pass two arguments into the reduce() callback function on line 1: the return item (called collectedValues) and the individual item. The return value, sometimes called the carry, is what makes reduce() unique. It can range from an integer to a collection such as Set.

The reduce() method itself on line 7 takes two values: the callback function and the initial value. Although the initial value is optional, it's usually included because you need something to hold the return values and, as a bonus, it gives other developers a clue about what they'll get back. The trickiest part of a reduce method is that the callback function must always return the carry item.

It's really worth reading the documentation to see more examples, but many of those examples are abstract ideas using numbers.[3] Consider a situation that's much more common: getting the unique values from an array.

You probably remember that this is a problem you already solved with Set in Tip 16, *Keep Unique Values with Set*, on page 69. You're absolutely correct, but you're going to expand on the solution to get several sets of unique values.

As in the previous example, you're going to get a list of unique values from a collection of dogs for an adoption website.

```
loops/reduce/reduce.js
const dogs = [
  {
    name: 'max',
    size: 'small',
    breed: 'boston terrier',
    color: 'black',
  },
  {
    name: 'don',
    size: 'large',
    breed: 'labrador',
    color: 'black',
  },
  {
    name: 'shadow',
    size: 'medium',
    breed: 'labrador',
    color: 'chocolate',
  },
];
```

If you want to see a few approaches using a for loop or Set directly, flip back to that earlier tip. For now, you'll jump right into getting the values with the reduce() method.

If all you wanted was the set of unique colors, you'd write a reduce method that loops through the objects checking the colors and saving the unique values.

---

3. https://developer.mozilla.org/en-US/docs/Web/JavaScript/Reference/Global_Objects/Array/Reduce

loops/reduce/reduce.js

```
Line 1  const colors = dogs.reduce((colors, dog) => {
     2    if (colors.includes(dog.color)) {
     3      return colors;
     4    }
     5    return [...colors, dog.color];
     6  }, []);
```

When you see a reduce method, the best place to start is at the end so you can see what kind of item you'll end up with. Remember that it can be any-thing— a string, a Boolean, an object. Make no assumptions.

If you look at line 6, you can see that you're initializing the function with an empty array.

The next trick to grasping a reduce function is understanding what the name of that initial value is after it enters the function. Generically, it's often called a "carry," but you can name it whatever you want because it's just a parameter. In this function on line 1, you name it something a little more revealing: colors.

Without going any further into the body of the function, you already know that you'll be getting back another array. That's valuable information, and it's the reason you should always start with an explicit carry value. You want the next developer to have as many clues as possible.

You have to be careful, though, because if you forget to return the carry value, it will effectively disappear. If you were to run the following function, you'd get a TypeError: Cannot read property 'includes' of undefined. When you forget to return the carry on line 5, the function will return undefined. This means the parameter colors is now undefined and doesn't have an includes() method.

loops/reduce/mistake.js

```
Line 1  const colors = dogs.reduce((colors, dog) => {
     2    if (colors.includes(dog.color)) {
     3      return colors;
     4    }
     5    [...colors, dog.color];
     6  }, []);
```

Moving in to the body of the initial unique colors function, you start to see the value of reduce() over other methods. On line 2, you check to see if the value is already in the array. If it is, no need to add it. Return the collection so far. If it's a new value, then you add it to the other colors on line 5 and return the updated array.

Let that sink in a moment. You're doing two things: You're returning a subset of data (changing the size) *and* you're returning modified data (changing the shape). More important, you're changing the size based on information contained inside the array itself. That's not something you can do with filter() or find().

Now here's the interesting part. Because you can change both the size and the shape of the data, you can recreate any other array method with reduce().

As a quick example, if you wanted to just get the colors of the dogs, you could use the map() method like this:

loops/reduce/map.js
```
const colors = dogs.map(dog => dog.color);
```

You could get the same value with a reduce function that takes an empty array to start and returns the array on every iteration.

loops/reduce/reduce.js
```
const colors = dogs.reduce((colors, dog) => {
  return [...colors, dog.color];
}, []);
```

As an exercise, try writing filter() and find() with reduce(). You'll learn about each of them in the process.

By no means should you rebuild methods in your code. Use the best tool for the job. Still, the fact that you can shows the power of reduce().

But back to our unique value reducer. You may be wondering why you should bother with a reducer at all when you just pass the results of the map() method in to Set and get the same result?

That's easy. Reducers give you the flexibility to handle more values with ease. And if you were getting the values for one set of properties, map() would make more sense. Remember that flexibility is good, but you should use it only when you've exhausted simpler options. When you need it, though, it's good to have.

For example, what if you wanted to get the unique values for *all* the keys in the dog object? You could run multiple map functions and pass those to Set. Or, you can use a reduce function that starts with empty sets and fills the objects in as you go.

There are many ways to do this, but the easiest would be to start with an object that contains empty sets. In the body of the reduce function, add each item to the set (remember that it will keep only the unique items). When you're finished, you have a collection of unique properties.

```
loops/reduce/reduce.js
const filters = dogs.reduce((filters, item) => {
  filters.breed.add(item.breed);
  filters.size.add(item.size);
  filters.color.add(item.color);
  return filters;
},
{
  breed: new Set(),
  size: new Set(),
  color: new Set(),
});
```

Now you have the benefit of keeping iterations low while also signaling the shape of the transformed data to other developers.

And it's precisely because you can change the size and shape of data that the possibilities are nearly endless.

Look at another example. In this case, you have a list of developers, and along with language specialty, you want a count by speciality.

```
loops/reduce/reduce.js
const developers = [
  {
    name: 'Jeff',
    language: 'php',
  },
  {
    name: 'Ashley',
    language: 'python',
  },
  {
    name: 'Sara',
    language: 'python',
  },
  {
    name: 'Joe',
    language: 'javascript',
  },
];
```

You could easily get a count by incrementing the language specialty on each iteration.

loops/reduce/reduce.js

```
const aggregated = developers.reduce((specialities, developer) => {
  const count = specialities[developer.language] || 0;
  return {
    ...specialities,
    [developer.language]: count + 1,
  };
}, {});
```

Notice that the initial value is just an empty object. In this case, you don't know what languages are going to be used so you'll need to add them dynamically. In case you're wondering: Yes, you can build this reduce function with Map instead of an object. Try it out and see what you come up with.

That's all for array methods. They provide a lot of value, and when you get comfortable with them, you'll appreciate how quickly you can reduce the lines of code while being even more transparent about the information you're returning. Don't be surprised that you turn to them more and more.

Still, there are times when normal for loops are the way to go. In the next tip, you'll look at a slight variation to the for loop called a for...in loop that lets you ignore all the annoying declarations of iterators and length by taking each item directly from the iterable.

Tip 27

Reduce Loop Clutter with for...in and for...each

In this tip, you'll learn how to maintain clarity with loops over iterables using for...in and over objects using for...of.

Hopefully by now you're convinced that array methods can handle most of your iterations in clear and predictable ways. Sometimes, however, an array method may be either inefficient or cumbersome.

There may be times you want to exit out of a loop when a result doesn't match what you need. In those cases, it makes no sense to keep iterating over information.

Alternatively, an array method may be overly complex when you're working with a collection that isn't an array. Remember that just because a structure isn't an array doesn't mean you can't use array methods. If you're working with an object, you can use Object.keys() to create an array of keys and then perform whatever method you want. Or you can use the spread operator to convert a Map to an array of pairs. If you need a refresher, head back to Tip 14, *Iterate Over Key-Value Data with Map and the Spread Operator*, on page 60.

In fact, those are great approaches. The popular Airbnb style guide, for example, insists that you always use array methods and restricts the use of the for...of and for...in loops.[4]

That opinion isn't shared by all. Sometimes it's not worth the hassle to convert structures to arrays and it's worth knowing other options.

Consider an application where you can select and compare multiple sets of information. Perhaps you're building an application that has a list of consulting firms. A user can select multiple firms and compare and contrast services.

Knowing what you know now, you'd probably use a Map to hold the various firms as users click on options. After all, you're constantly adding and deleting information, which is an action a Map can handle easily.

---

4. https://github.com/airbnb/javascript/issues/851

As the user clicks on firms they're interested in, you could add the firms to a simple map that uses the ID of the firm as a key and the name of the firm as the value.

loops/for/for.js

```
const firms = new Map()
  .set(10, 'Ivie Group')
  .set(23, 'Soundscaping Source')
  .set(31, 'Big 6');
```

You can do a lot with that small amount of information. You could select details from a database. You could check availability or create a comparison chart. In all cases, you'd need to act on the collection one piece at a time.

For this example, loop through the firms a user has selected to check and see if they're available. (For the purposes of this example, you'll use a generic isAvailable() function that would be defined elsewhere.) If one isn't available, return a message saying the firm is unavailable. Otherwise, return a message saying all are available.

If you try writing this out, you'll immediately notice a problem. You can't use a traditional for loop because the collection isn't an array. You can easily bypass that problem by converting the map to an array with the spread operator before looping.

loops/for/traditional.js

```
const entries = [...firms];
for (let i = 0; i < entries.length; i++) {
  const [id, name] = entries[i];
  if (!isAvailable(id)) {
    return `${name} is not available`;
  }
}
return 'All firms are available';
```

That loop is pretty straightforward. It gets the information you need in a fairly transparent way. By now, though, you know there are better ways to loop. And you probably noticed that because you have to convert to an array, you might as well use an array method.

But there's no good array method to perform the action. Sure, there are plenty of options that you could try. You might use find() to see if there's a firm that's unavailable.

```
loops/for/full.js
const unavailable = [...firms].find(firm => {
  const [id] = firm;
  return !isAvailable(id);
});

if (unavailable) {
  return `${unavailable[1]} is not available`;
}

return 'All firms are available';
```

You might also write a reduce() method that returns a string with the success message as a default.

```
loops/for/full.js
const message = [...firms].reduce((availability, firm) => {
  const [id, name] = firm;
  if (!isAvailable(id)) {
    return `${name} is not available`;
  }
  return availability;
}, 'All firms are available');
return message;
```

There are many ways to solve the problem. Maybe those solutions are fine for you and your team. Still, they're a little clunky. You'd probably have to read them twice to understand what's happening.

The problem is the find() approach is a two-step process (find if there are unavailable firms, and then build a message), and the reduce() approach is a little difficult to understand.

There's also the problem that the find() function will give you only the first unavailable firm and the reduce() function will give you only the last.

To be fair, you won't solve that problem here. Try to find a solution both with array methods and with other loops. (Hint: Chain filter() and map() to make an array of messages.) For now, however, ignore that optimization and focus instead on whether all are available or not.

You've seen three ways to solve the exact same problem with the same result. They all share a common feature: They all require you to first convert the map to an array. Turns out that's not even necessary. The property on the Map that lets you use the spread operator, the MapIterator, is the same property that will let you iterate over a map directly.

In the tip on using the spread operator with Map, you learned about the MapIterator. It's just a specific instance of the more generalized Iterator, which designates a specific type of object that can access pieces one at a time. You can find them on maps, arrays, and sets, and you can even make your own, as you'll see in Tip 41, *Create Iterable Properties with Generators*, on page 192.

Most important, you can use the iterator with a special loop called a for...of loop. This loop is very similar to the for loop except that you don't iterate over the indexes (that let i = 0 part). Instead, you loop directly over the members of the collection.

In the loop parameters, you declare a name for the individual item and then use that in the body.

Instead of converting a specialized object to an array, you use the exact same idea of a for loop while removing reference to indexes. You effectively use the callback method from an array method. Here's a translation of the functions you saw earlier.

loops/for/for.js
```
for (const firm of firms) {
  const [id, name] = firm;
  if (!isAvailable(id)) {
    return `${name} is not available`;
  }
}
return 'All firms are available';
```

Notice a few things: First, you declare the variable, firm with const. Because const is block scoped, this variable won't exist outside the loop so you don't have to worry about polluting the rest of the code. Next, using the same ideas from array methods, you act on the item directly. You don't need to reference the full collection as you do with entries[i] in the for loop. It's a combination of array callback methods and for loops.

As a bonus, you also gain a slight optimization by not converting an iterable to an array before then iterating over it again. You don't have to avoid array methods to gain that micro-optimization, but it's something to consider.

What are the trade-offs? The most obvious is that because the loop can do anything, you lose some predictability. Honestly, that's about the only problem as long as you don't mutate the collection as you loop through it (which you could easily do). But you can mutate collections with array methods, too. Avoiding side effects and mutations requires discipline more than syntax.

With all those advantages you may wonder, should you always loop directly? In short, no. As a rule, use array methods when they're clear fits and you prefer them as the default. When you're filtering data in a map, for example, you should use filters. When you're converting a map to an array of values, use the map() method. Otherwise, you'll be stuck creating a container array and mutating it on each loop. Use for...of when it makes the most sense.

There's another slight complication—or benefit, depending on how you think about it—to for...of loops. There's a similar but different loop that only works on key-value objects. It's called the for...in loop.

The for...in loop is very similar to the for...of loop. You don't need to convert an object's keys to an array with Object.keys() because you operate directly on the object itself. Specifically, you loop over the properties of an object.

If you've worked with JavaScript objects in-depth, you'll likely know there are some complications with object properties because they can be inherited from other objects in a prototype chain. In addition, objects have non-enumerable properties that are also skipped during iteration.

In short, properties on objects can be complex. You can read more about it on the Mozilla Developer Network.[5]

Most times, though, you're working with simple things, and that's what you'll focus on here. To start off, convert your map of firms to an object. It's almost identical, but because keys have to be strings, you'll need to convert them from numbers. In reality, you can use numbers as keys in object literal syntax and they'll be covertly converted to strings, but that's a problem with objects, not an advantage.

loops/for/forin.js
```js
const firms = {
  '10': 'Ivie Group',
  '23': 'Soundscaping Source',
  '31': 'Big 6',
};
```

When using a for...in loop, you'll get each property one at a time. Unlike the for...of loop, you don't get the values, and you'll have to reference the full collection using the key on each iteration. Everything else should be familiar. You name the variable, preferably with const, and then you use that in the body, knowing it will change on each iteration.

Try and convert the last for...of loop and see what you get.

You probably came up with something like this:

---

5. https://developer.mozilla.org/en-US/docs/Web/JavaScript/Reference/Statements/for...in#Iterating_over_own_properties_only

loops/for/forin.js
```
for (const id in firms) {
  if (!isAvailable(parseInt(id, 10))) {
    return `${firms[id]} is not available`;
  }
}
return 'All firms are available';
```

Because you're getting the property and not a pair, you don't need to extract the name and value separately. Any time you need the value, you can grab it using array notation on the individual item. If you need the key to be an integer, which you do in this case, you'll need to convert it using parseInt(). This is why the subtle conversions that happen with object keys can be so confusing.

As with the for...of loop, use the for...in loop when it makes sense, but try not to use it as the default. If you're only going to use the keys, it may make more sense to pull them out with Object.keys() before using an array method. The same is true if you just plan on using the values. You can use Object.values() to convert those to an array, though that's less common.

One other precaution: Don't mutate the object as you loop over it. That can be very dangerous, and bugs can creep in quickly, especially if you add or modify properties other than the property currently being iterated.

Now you have a whole new set of tools for iterating over collections. As you saw in this example, you can solve most problems with multiple methods, so it often comes down to a matter of personal and team preference. Over time, you'll find that you prefer some methods over the others, and that's fine. There are fewer right and wrong answers in development than people think.

In the next chapter, you'll be moving from the nuts and bolts of working with data into composing functions. You'll start with simply exploring new ways of working with parameters. And yes, there are enough changes that we'll need a whole chapter to explore them. JavaScript can do a lot of interesting things with functions, so it's exciting that even simple parameters are now more flexible. This is where the fun really begins.

CHAPTER 6

Clean Up Parameters and Return Statements

I'm famous for assuming I can always find a shortcut. If I'm driving down the highway and hit construction, I'll take the first off ramp, determined to find a quick way around the delay. Exiting the highway requires that I ignore the protests of my wife, who thinks it would just be easier to slow down and follow the orange cones.

Well, my wife is usually right. I pull off and take a side road that suddenly veers even further off course. I don't mind. I grew up in the middle of nowhere, so I have an intuition for county roads. At least I think I do, until the paved road turns into a dirt road before coming to a dead end at a wheat field. Giving in, I take out my phone to turn on the GPS. Oh wait. I'm in the middle of a wheat field. There's no signal.

Simple actions can spiral out of control quickly. This happens all the time with function arguments. You start with the best of intentions. The function will take two arguments and return a simple value. Suddenly, edge cases pop up. Data inconsistencies creep in. Before you know it, you need eight different parameters to cover dozens of situations. You'd like to give up, but by now, you're too afraid of breaking all the code downstream that depends on this function.

In this chapter, you'll learn how to plan for changing function arguments and how to create parameters that will be clean and give you flexibility.

First, you'll see how to add default parameters to cover situations where information may not be available. Next, you'll learn how to pull information out of objects using destructuring and how destructuring can be combined with function parameters to accommodate a range of options. Using that knowledge, you'll combine information back into new objects, creating return statements that share plenty of information in usable bundles. After that, you'll return to parameters to see how you can create functions without even knowing the number of arguments to expect.

There's no problem with being adventurous as long as you have a plan for the inevitable contingencies. In this chapter, you'll see how functions can be built to handle unexpected changes. Learn the lesson I never did as a driver: Leap into the unknown, but plan for the unforeseen.

Tip 28

Create Default Parameters

In this tip, you'll learn how to use default parameters to set values when a parameter is absent.

No matter how much planning you do, things change. This is especially true of function parameters. When you write a function, you expect a few parameters. Then, as code grows and edge cases emerge, suddenly the parameters you supplied aren't enough.

In the next several tips, you'll learn different techniques for handling parameters. Nearly all of these techniques can help you cope in some way with changing requirements. But to start, you'll learn the easiest trick: setting default parameters.

Consider a basic helper function. All you want to do is convert pounds to kilograms. That seems simple. You simply need to take the weight as an input and divide the weight in pounds by 2.2 to get kilograms. (Apologies to non-Americans who don't have to deal with this silliness. I'm sure you also get stuck converting other measurements.)

params/defaults/simple.js
```
function convertWeight(weight) {
  return weight / 2.2;
}
```

That code seems easy enough. And you use it throughout the app. Before you know it, a ticket comes in because someone needs to be able to pass ounces. And because there are 16 ounces in a pound, you'll need to convert that number to a decimal before adding it to the pounds.

Fine. You add in a parameter for ounces, but now you're in a bind. Do you track down every instance of the function and add in a zero for the ounces? Or do you try to handle cases where a value wasn't provided?

You can try the first approach and update every function, but there's always the chance that you'll miss one. Fortunately, in JavaScript, you don't need to pass all the parameters to a function. They can be optional. If you're missing a parameter, the value is set to undefined.

Knowing that, you go for the second approach and add a little bit of code to set the value if it doesn't exist.

params/defaults/more.js
```
function convertWeight(weight, ounces) {
  const oz = ounces ? ounces / 16 : 0;
  const total = weight + oz;
  return total / 2.2;
}
```

When you run convertWeight(44,11), you get 20.3125, which isn't bad, but nearly every other conversion returns a long decimal string. convertWeight(44, 8) returns 20.22727....

Stranger still, when you run convertWeight(6.6), you expect to get 3 and instead you get 2.999999.... You can thank floating point arithmetic for that.[1]

Great—now you need to round up to handle cases where the floating point arithmetic doesn't match user expectations. And because you're rounding anyway, you should make the number of decimal points an option, too, with a default of two decimal places.

You add some more code to handle the missing parameter. You also add in a helper function, roundTo, to handle the rounding (see the book code for implementation details).

But there's a complication. To make the default two decimal places, you can't just check to see if the parameter roundTo is truthy. You can't, for example, write const round = roundTo || 2; because if the user were to pass in 0 as the number of decimal places they wanted, it would default to falsy and go back to two places.

Instead, you'd have to explicitly check that the value was undefined, which means that no value was submitted.

params/defaults/problem.js
```
function convertWeight(weight, ounces, roundTo) {
  const oz = ounces / 16 || 0;
  const total = weight + oz;
  const conversion = total / 2.2;

  const round = roundTo === undefined ? 2 : roundTo;

  return roundToDecimalPlace(conversion, round);
}
```

---

1. https://docs.oracle.com/cd/E19957-01/806-3568/ncg_goldberg.html

Every time, the function becomes a little more complex. That's unavoidable in a world with changing requirements. What you don't want to do is create problems by having undefined variables. That means every time you add a new parameter, you end up adding a new ternary or short circuiting to create a default value.

Changing requirements are part of life. There's nothing any syntax can do about that. But you can minimize a bunch of variable checks with default parameters.

All this means is that if the value isn't passed, it takes the placeholder value. It's that simple. You've probably seen it in countless other languages. You define the default parameter by putting an equal sign (=) after the parameter name along with the value. If there's no value for that parameter, it falls back to the default.

The updated function still has the additional logic to handle the new requirements (adding ounces, rounding decimals), but at least you can be confident you'll get something.

params/defaults/default.js
```
function convertWeight(weight, ounces = 0, roundTo = 2) {
  const total = weight + (ounces / 16);
  const conversion = total / 2.2;

  return roundToDecimalPlace(conversion, roundTo);
}
```

As a bonus, you give a clue to other developers that you're looking for a particular data type. They'd know, for example, that ounces is an integer. This isn't a substitute for a proper type system, but it's a nice little extra.

JavaScript and Type Checking

You don't need a type system, but if you like one, there are more options now than ever. The most obvious example is TypeScript, which is a superset of JavaScript (it includes all of JavaScript and then some). It's a good tool, and it's popular with developers who love a good type system.

If you want to write ordinary JavaScript but with a type system, you should check out flow, a static type system developed by Facebook.[a] It's flexible enough to incorporate into individual files, giving you a chance to try types without having to fully switch over to TypeScript.

---

a.   https://flow.org

Default parameters aren't a perfect solution. Parameter order still matters. If you didn't want to include ounces but you did want to specify the number of decimal points, you would still need to clarify the number—in this case, it would be 0.

params/defaults/default.js
```
convertWeight(4, 0, 2);
```

If you absolutely don't want to pass in a value, you can pass in undefined and the function would use the default parameter, but use this approach with caution. It's too easy to make mistakes when you pass in undefined. If you passed in null, for example, you wouldn't get the default value. Besides, if you really don't care what the default is, you should just use the value set as the default parameter. It's more clear to others reading the code and it's less likely to break later if the function changes slightly.

params/defaults/default.js
```
convertWeight(4, undefined, 2);
```

A common way around this problem is to pass an object as a second parameter. Because an object can have multiple key-value pairs, you won't need to change the function parameters every time a new option is added. You will, however, need to pull the information from the object.

In the next tip, you'll see how it's easier to use objects in parameters by pulling out data with destructuring.

Access Object Properties with Destructuring

In this tip, you'll learn how to pull information out of objects and arrays quickly with destructuring.

In the previous tip, you learned how to create default parameters, which are a great addition to the language, but they still have one big problem: Parameters always have to be given in order. If you wanted to specify the third parameter but you didn't care about the second, you'd still be forced to enter a value. Default parameters aren't helpful if you want to skip a parameter.

What about situations where you need a large number of arguments for a function? What about situations where you know that the needs of a functions are likely to change? In JavaScript, most developers add extra arguments to an object and pass the object as the last parameter to a function.

For example, what if you wanted to display a number of photos and needed to translate the values into an HTML string? Specifically, you want to include the image, title, photographer, and location in that order in your string, but you also want any additional information. Some photographs include equipment, image type, lenses information, and any other customizations. You don't know what it all will be, but you still want to display it.

There is a lot of information associated with a photograph. Passing that information as individual parameters would be excessive—you could end up with about ten parameters. Besides, the information is already structured. What's the point in changing it? Here's an example of some information about a photograph.

```
params/destructuring/destructuring.js
const landscape = {
  title: 'Landscape',
  photographer: 'Nathan',
  equipment: 'Canon',
  format: 'digital',
  src: '/landscape-nm.jpg',
  location: [32.7122222, -103.1405556],
};
```

In this case, it makes sense to pass the whole photo object directly into a function. Of course, once you have it in the function, what do you do with it?

You can either pull the information directly from the object when needed using dot syntax—photo.title—or you can assign the information to variables and then use the variables later in the code.

Getting the values you know ahead of time is easy. The real trick is getting the excess information—information that you don't know about ahead of time. The only way to get it is to remove the key-value pairs you're using elsewhere and then keep whatever is leftover.

Fortunately, you're smart enough to know that you should copy the object before mutating it (good work). And after you copy it, you can delete the keys you don't need one at a time. The end result is a lot of object assignments for a very small action. Nearly two-thirds of the function is pulling information from an object.

params/destructuring/problem.js
```
function displayPhoto(photo) {
  const title = photo.title;
  const photographer = photo.photographer || 'Anonymous';
  const location = photo.location;
  const url = photo.src;

  const copy = { ...photo };
  delete copy.title;
  delete copy.photographer;
  delete copy.location;
  delete copy.src;

  const additional = Object.keys(copy).map(key => `${key}: ${copy[key]}`);

  return (`
    <img alt="Photo of ${title} by ${photographer}" src="${url}" />
    <div>${title}</div>
    <div>${photographer}</div>
    <div>Latitude: ${location[0]} </div>
    <div>Longitude: ${location[1]} </div>
    <div>${additional.join(' <br/> ')}</div>
  `);
}
```

Remember back in Tip 10, *Use Objects for Static Key-Value Lookups*, on page 41 where you learned that objects are great for passing around static information? You're about to learn why.

In JavaScript, you can assign variables directly from an object using a process called destructuring assignment.

It works like this: Destructuring allows you to create a variable with the same name as an object's key assigned with the value from the object.

As usual, it's always easier to see. In this case, you have an object with a key of photographer and you're going to create a variable named photographer from that object.

```
const landscape = {
  photographer: 'Nathan',
};
const { photographer } = landscape;
photographer
// Nathan
```

Notice a few things. First, you still have to declare a variable type. As usual, you should prefer const. Second, the assignment variable must match the key in the object. Finally, it's set against the object. You are merely assigning a variable. The curly braces merely signal the value that variable should use is inside an object.

That's the bare bones—set a variable using the key. Of course, nothing is ever that simple. What happens when a key doesn't exist? Well, in that case, the value is merely undefined, but you can also set a default value while destructuring.

```
const landscape = {
};
const { photographer = 'Anonymous', title} = landscape;

photographer
// Anonymous

title
// undefined
```

At this point, you've caught up to regular parameters. You can set a variable from a key. You can set default values. But what do you do if you don't know the key name? How do you get the leftover information? Remember that you want any additional information from a photograph and you have no clue what that will be.

Good news: Your favorite three dots are back. You can collect any additional values into a new variable using three dots (...) followed by the variable name. When you use the three-dot syntax to collect information, it's no longer called the spread operator. It's called the rest operator, and you'll see more of it in upcoming tips.

You can name the variable anything you want. It doesn't need to match a key (in fact, it shouldn't match a key). And the value of the variable will be an object of the remaining key-value pairs.

```
const landscape = {
  photographer: 'Nathan',
  equipment: 'Canon',
  format: 'digital',
};
j
const {
    photographer,
    ...additional
} = landscape;

additional;
// { equipment: 'Canon', format: 'digital'}
```

photographer is pulled out from the object, and the remaining fields go into a new object. You essentially copied the photograph object and deleted the photographer key.

Notice how the variable assignments are on different lines: photographer is on one line and ...additional is on the next. It's simply a style preference to keep things more readable. You can keep both assignments on the same line as you do above.

Now you can pull information from an object, assign default parameters, and collect additional key-values. As if that weren't enough to celebrate, you can also assign a key to a different variable name. This is useful in situations where the key name is taken by a previously defined variable or you just don't like the key name and you want something more expressive.

In the original code, you assign the information from photo.src to the variable name url. To accomplish that with destructuring, you simply put the key name first with a colon followed by the value you want to assign it to.

```
const landscape = {
  src: '/landscape-nm.jpg',
};

const { src: url } = landscape;
src
// ReferenceError: src is not defined
url
// '/landscape-nm.jpg'
```

You still must use the key name to signal which value you want to use, but you are not bound to that key name.

Finally, you can also use destructuring assignment with arrays, with one big exception: Because there are no keys in arrays, you can use any variable name you want, but you must assign the information in order. If you want to assign the third item to a variable, you must first assign the previous two values to a variable. Otherwise, it's simple. Destructuring is a great way to work with array pairs in a situation where the order denotes some information. For example, if you had an array of latitude and longitude, you'd always know the first value corresponds to latitude and the second to longitude.

```
const landscape = {
  location: [32.7122222, -103.1405556],
};

const { location } = landscape;
const [latitude, longitude] = location
latitude
// 32.7122222
longitude
// -103.1405556
```

Of course, in the preceding situation, you pulled out location first from an object and then latitude and longitude from the array. There's no need to make it a two-step process. You can combine the assignments during destructuring.

```
const landscape = {
  location: [32.7122222, -103.1405556],
};

const { location: [latitude, longitude] } = landscape;
latitude
// 32.7122222
longitude
// -103.1405556
```

All right, that was a lot to think about. But it really can clean things up fast. Remember the original function? Here it is with destructuring:

params/destructuring/alternate.js
```
function displayPhoto(photo) {
  const {
    title,
    photographer = 'Anonymous',
    location: [latitude, longitude],
    src: url,
    ...other
  } = photo;
  const additional = Object.keys(other).map(key => `${key}: ${other[key]}`);
```

```
  return (`
    <img alt="Photo of ${title} by ${photographer}" src="${url}" />
    <div>${title}</div>
    <div>${photographer}</div>
    <div>Latitude: ${latitude} </div>
    <div>Longitude: ${longitude} </div>
    <div>${additional.join(' <br/> ')}</div>
  `);
}
```

Looks good, doesn't it? But you're probably wondering what this is doing in a chapter about cleaning up parameters.

The best part about destructuring is that you can move it right into the parameters of a function. The information will be assigned just as it was in the body of the function, but there's no need to declare the variable type. If you're curious, it'll be assigned with let so it's possible to reassign the variable.

In other words, you can clean up the original code even more:

params/destructuring/destructuring.js
```
function displayPhoto({
  title,
  photographer = 'Anonymous',
  location: [latitude, longitude],
  src: url,
  ...other
}) {
  const additional = Object.keys(other).map(key => `${key}: ${other[key]}`);
  return (`
    <img alt="Photo of ${title} by ${photographer}" src="${url}" />
    <div>${title}</div>
    <div>${photographer}</div>
    <div>Latitude: ${latitude} </div>
    <div>Longitude: ${longitude} </div>
    <div>${additional.join(' <br/> ')}</div>
  `);
}
```

Notice that you still need the curly braces, but otherwise everything is the same. Now when you call the function, you can just pass the object and everything will be assigned to the proper parameters: displayPhoto(landscape).

Not only did you save yourself all the assignment problems, but by passing an object as a parameter, you don't have to worry about the order of the key-values.

And if you wanted to pull out another key-value, it's just a matter of adding the new variable to the destructuring. Say you wanted to assign equipment explicitly. All you need to do is add in the new variable name in the list of variables and you'll be good to go. There's no need to worry about other times when the function is called. If equipment isn't part of another object, it will merely be undefined.

That was probably a whirlwind, but it should give you a taste for how easily you can pull information from objects. The only downside is this only works on objects used as key-value pairs or object instances of a class.

Destructuring won't work on Map, which is fine because this is primarily useful when you're sending information between functions, meaning you shouldn't be looping or reassigning values. In other words, the data is static, so an object is a great choice.

As if that wasn't overwhelming enough, you've only seen half of it. In the next tip, you're going to go in the other direction and put information back into an object.

Tip 30

Simplify Key-Value Assignment

In this tip, you'll learn how to make objects quickly with shortened key-value assignment.

You just learned how to pull apart objects in a clear and clean way. Now that you have all those pieces laying out on your proverbial work bench, you need to put them back together. It wouldn't be any good if the writers of the spec gave you a clean interface to take objects apart while leaving you no way to put them back together.

Well, you're in luck. The same technique you'd use to take objects apart works in reverse. It's time to build new objects using similar syntax that will leave your code clear and predictable.

Start with a similar object of photo information:

params/assignment/assignment.js
```
const landscape = {
  title: 'Landscape',
  photographer: 'Nathan',
  location: [32.7122222, -103.1405556],
};
```

In this case, you have the location information in latitude and longitude, but what you need is the city and state names.

Elsewhere in the code, you have a helper function that looks up regional information (city, state, county) from the geographical coordinates. The implementation details aren't important. What matters here is that you get back another object of information.

params/assignment/assignment.js
```
const region = {
  city: 'Hobbs',
  county: 'Lea',
  state: {
    name: 'New Mexico',
    abbreviation: 'NM',
  },
};
```

Now you just need to take the city and state from the return object and assign it to the new object. Fortunately, adding information into objects is very simple.

If you want to add a key-value pair to an object where the key is the same name as the variable, simply put in the variable. That's it. You don't need any extra colons.

You can also mix it up—have some key-value pairs defined with a variable and some defined the traditional way.

```
params/assignment/assignment.js
function getCityAndState({ location }) {
  const { city, state } = determineCityAndState(location);
  return {
    city,
    state: state.abbreviation,
  };
  // {
  //   city: 'Hobbs',
  //   state: 'NM'
  // }
}
```

In this case, you're adding a key of city with destructuring assignment and a key of state with normal key-value assignment.

What if you just want to sub out one piece of information in an object but keep everything else? For example, say you want to use getCityAndState() to translate the coordinates into strings, but you want to keep everything else from the original object.

You can combine the object spread operator with regular key-value assignment to swap out one piece of information while retaining everything else.

```
params/assignment/assignment.js
function setRegion({ location, ...details }) {
  const { city, state } = determineCityAndState(location);
  return {
    city,
    state: state.abbreviation,
    ...details,
  };
}
```

Don't gloss over this code too quickly. There's actually something interesting happening. When you use destructuring to pull out the location key-value pair, you're also assigning everything else *except* location to the variable name details. You're essentially copying the object and then running delete photo.location.

When you recombine the object by spreading out details along with new key value pairs, you're doing some subtle but powerful manipulation of objects to get exactly the information you want.

The result will have no location, but it will include all the original information along with the city and state.

```
params/assignment/assignment.js
{
  title: 'Landscape',
  photographer: 'Nathan',
  city: 'Hobbs',
  state: 'NM',
};
```

As you know, the spread operator is my favorite ES6 feature. But I know several developers who say destructuring is their favorite feature and that it's changed the way they work with objects and functions. It will change the way you work, too.

Now that you have the tools you need to pull objects apart and put them back together, be sure to think twice before you create objects by assigning each key-value explicitly. If you're going to assign a value to a variable, you might as well use the key name. Before long, destructuring will become second nature, and you'll love how it transforms your code.

In the next tip, you'll learn how to have a variable number of parameters with rest parameters using your favorite three-dot syntax.

Tip 31

Pass a Variable Number of Arguments with the Rest Operator

In this tip, you'll learn to collect an unknown number of parameters with the rest operator.

In the previous tips, you saw how object destructuring would let you combine several parameters into a single argument.

Using objects to hold parameters is a great technique, but it's really only useful in situations where the parameters are different and you know them ahead of time. In other words, it only makes sense in situations with objects.

That may seem obvious, but it raises the question: How do you handle an unknown number of similar parameters?

Think back to the photo display application. What if you wanted to allow your users to tag photos but you only wanted the tags to be a certain length? You could easily write a very short validation function that takes a size and an array of tags and returns true if all are valid.

params/rest/simple.js
```
function validateCharacterCount(max, items) {
  return items.every(item => item.length < max);
}
```

Notice the every() method? It's another simple array method you haven't seen before. As with filter(), you pass a callback that returns a truthy or falsy value. The every() method returns true if every item in an array passed to the callback returns truthy. Otherwise, it returns false.

Running the function is simple. Just pass in an array of strings.

params/rest/simple.js
```
validateCharacterCount(10, ['Hobbs', 'Eagles']);
// true
```

This code is great because it's so generic. You can easily reuse it elsewhere. The only down side to this code is that it locks the users of your function into a particular collection type. Another developer might, for example, want to test that a single username isn't too long. To use the code, they'd have to know that they'd need to pass an array. If they didn't, they would get an error.

params/rest/simple.js

```
  validateCharacterCount(10, 'wvoquine');
// TypeError: items.every is not a function
```

You could write some documentation to communicate the parameters, but there's a better way. Previously, JavaScript developers solved this problem by using the built-in arguments object. This handy object gives you an array-like collection of all the arguments that are passed to a function.

params/rest/problem.js

```
function getArguments() {
  return arguments;
}
getArguments('Bloomsday', 'June 16');
// { '0': 'Bloomsday', '1': 'June 16' }
```

You may have noticed the phrase "array-like." Unfortunately, arguments is an object, so you'll need to do some converting to get it to an array. Specifically, you'll need to statically call a method on the Array object (as opposed to an array instance) as you see in line 2 in the code that follows. This line of code takes all arguments after the first one, the character count, and combines them into an array.

params/rest/problem.js

```
Line 1 function validateCharacterCount(max) {
     2   const items = Array.prototype.slice.call(arguments, 1);
     3   return items.every(item => item.length < max);
     4 }
```

Now you can pass as many arguments as you want knowing you'll have an array inside the function.

What about situations where you already have an array? Because you are converting the arguments into an array, you'll need to convert your array into a list of arguments.

Think back to when you learned about the spread operator. At the time, you learned you always need to spread into something. Up until now, you've only spread it into another array. You can also spread it as a list of parameters. In other words, when you collect parameters into a list, you can easily handle cases of strings or arrays.

Using these techniques, you can now use your function with a variety of parameters.

params/rest/problem.js
```
validateCharacterCount(10, 'wvoquie');
// true

const tags = ['Hobbs', 'Eagles'];
validateCharacterCount(10, ...tags);
// true
```

This is more flexible, but it's far from perfect. The biggest problem is that the syntax to work with the arguments object is a little convoluted. As a result, few developers (except the most hard-core JavaScript developers) used it. Not to mention that when you use the arguments object, there are absolutely no clues in the function parameters that you accept a list of arguments. Another developer would have to dig into the function body to understand what they can pass to the function.

Enter rest parameters. Rest parameters enable you to pass a list of arguments and assigns them to a variable.

JavaScript and Functional Languages

JavaScript was highly influenced by a variety of languages including Java (an object-oriented language), Scheme (a lisp or functional language), and Self (a prototype language).[a] This means that JavaScript can handle multiple paradigms. As a result, JavaScript is a great environment to explore ideas from other paradigms, especially concepts from functional languages.

You've already explored a number of functional concepts such as pure functions, side effects, and currying. Rest arguments themselves are a carryover from Lisp dialects (such as Scheme). You'll see even more functional concepts when you explore higher-order functions. JavaScript is a great way to break out of an object-oriented mold to try new ideas.

_____
a.   https://www.youtube.com/watch?v=DogGMNBZZvg

You declare rest operators using your favorite three dots (...) followed by the variable you'd like to assign them to. Any parameters passed beyond that point are collected into the variable as an array.

params/rest/rest.js
```
function getArguments(...args) {
  return args;
}
getArguments('Bloomsday', 'June 16');
// ['Bloomsday', 'June 16']
```

It's that simple. Try rewriting the validateCharacterCount() function using rest arguments.

It probably took you no time at all to come up with this:

params/rest/rest.js
```
function validateCharacterCount(max, ...items) {
  return items.every(item => item.length < max);
}
```

In addition to being simpler and cleaner, it is more predictable. Now a developer can tell that this function takes at minimum two arguments. Even those unfamiliar with the rest operator have enough clues that a quick Stack Overflow search would fill in the details.

You'd call the function exactly the same way as you did with the previous function, by either passing a list of arguments or spreading an array of arguments into a list. This is no different from the previous code when you used the arguments object.

params/rest/rest.js
```
validateCharacterCount(10, 'wvoquie');
// true

validateCharacterCount(10, ...['wvoquie']);
// true

const tags = ['Hobbs', 'Eagles'];
validateCharacterCount(10, ...tags);
// true

validateCharacterCount(10, 'Hobbs', 'Eagles');
// true
```

At this point, you've accounted for a situation where you might get either a list or an array. There are a few other reasons you might use rest arguments.

First, you want to signal to other developers that you'll be working with arguments as an array. In the absence of type checking, this is another little clue that will help future developers. A lot of developers will use the rest operator even though the data they're passing in will be in the form of an array. Even though they always spread in the information when calling the function, it's a clear marker of the expected parameter type.

Second, the rest operator can give you a nice way to debug code. For example, it can help you decode library functions that you suspect may be getting additional parameters, and you can use a rest argument to collect any lingering arguments.

You've worked with the map() method several times, and you know the callback function takes the item being checked as an argument. It turns out that the callback function passes a few more arguments after the individual items. If you collect the rest of the parameters and log them, you'll see the map() operator also takes the index of the item being checked and the full collection.

params/rest/rest.js
```
['Spirited Away', 'Princess Mononoke'].map((film, ...other) => {
  console.log(other);
  return film.toLowerCase();
});
// [0, ['Spirited Away', 'Princess Mononoke']]
// [1, ['Spirited Away', 'Princess Mononoke']]
```

This isn't a big deal on the map() operator, which is well-documented, but the rest operator can help you see parameters that you might not have otherwise known about. The rest operator is a great way to debug.

Third, rest arguments are a great way to pass props through functions if you have no plans to alter them.

This is nice when you want to wrap a couple of functions and pass the arguments through. For example, you may have a modal, and when changes are saved, you'll want to close a modal while simultaneously updating some information with another function.

params/rest/rest.js
```
function applyChanges(...args) {
  updateAccount(...args);
  closeModal();
}
```

Finally, don't forget the rest operator isn't just for parameters. As you've seen, it works for pulling the remaining key-values from objects or the remaining values from arrays.

Much like the spread operator, you can recreate a common array method while removing side effects. If you wanted to recreate the shift() method, which returns the first item of an array and removes that item from the original array, simply combine the rest operator and destructuring.

params/rest/rest.js
```
const queue = ['stop', 'collaborate', 'listen'];
const [first, ...remaining] = queue;
first;
// 'stop'
remaining;
// ['collaborate', 'listen'];
```

You get the first value and an array of the remaining values. As a bonus, the original array is still intact.

The only downside to using the rest operator as an argument is that it must be the last argument in all situations. It must be the last parameter for a function. It must be the last value when destructuring. This means that although you can recreate the shift() method—return the first item—you can't recreate the pop() method, which returns the last item of an array.

```
const [...beginning, last] = queue;
// SyntaxError: Rest element must be last element
```

Still, the rest operator is very useful, and you'll find lots of opportunities to work it into your code.

Look at how much more you can do with functions already. And you've only just begun. In the next chapter, you'll move beyond parameters and return statements and explore how to construct more powerful and flexible functions.

CHAPTER 7

Build Flexible Functions

Several years ago, the *New York Times* asked a master furniture builder to review furniture from Ikea, Target, and other discount retailers.[1]

Unsurprisingly, the craftsman was not impressed. He noticed problems with the wood finish, screws that would tear out, and other issues. Astonishingly, he noticed a piece of chipping paint and concluded that the piece was painted before it was cut and that the blade cutting the wood was dull. A single piece of chipped paint told him something about the construction process and the tools used to create it.

A master of his or her craft can see things that others don't. In this chapter, you're going to learn to master functions, and in the process, you'll see ideas in code that you've probably never considered before. Problems disappear and new ideas pop up regularly.

Functions are so common that it's easy to ignore them. But functions in JavaScript are different. You may think you know how to use them, but you'll be surprised to find how much more they are capable of. This chapter isn't about the basics. It's about how you can use functions in ways you may not have explored before.

You'll start off by learning how to write testable code. Testable functions are more clean and easy to maintain, but learning to write them takes a little effort. From there, you'll return to arrow functions to see how you can take all the ideas from parameters and apply them in single line functions. Next, you'll dive into higher-order functions—functions that return functions—and learn two techniques to help you lock in information to make clear, reusable functions. Finally, you'll return to arrow functions to see how you can use

---

1. http://www.nytimes.com/2005/10/20/garden/cheap-its-chic-but-is-it-good.html

them to solve a sneaky context problem that will drive you crazy if you aren't expecting it.

Functions, currying, higher-order functions. These are the concepts that turn casual JavaScript writers into fanatics. They're the concepts I love most about the language.

When you're finished, you'll see problems in new ways. You won't be baffled when this returns undefined. You'll see a context problem that you can solve with arrow functions. When a variable is inaccessible, you'll see an opportunity for closures. Masters of a craft see the world differently. When you're finished mastering functions, you'll see all problems in a new way.

Tip 32

Write Functions for Testability

I had a literature professor who said that classes about writing don't include enough reading and classes about reading don't include enough writing. The same is true of code and tests: Books about code don't talk enough about testing and books about testing don't talk enough about composing code.

Time to fix that. Testing is important. If you don't do it, you should. It makes your code easier to refactor. It makes legacy code much easier to understand. And it generally results in cleaner, less buggy applications.

Most developers agree with this. Why then is testing neglected?

It's simple. Writing tests is hard. Or more accurately, many developers think writing tests is hard because they try to fit tests onto their existing code. And their existing code is tightly coupled with external dependencies.

Code that's hard to test is often unnecessarily complex. Instead of struggling to make tests for your code, you should focus on writing code that is testable. Your code will improve, your tests will be easier to write, and the user experience will be identical. There's nothing to lose.

If you're new to testing, check the documentation for one of three popular testing frameworks—jasmine,[2] mocha,[3] or jest[4]—for some quick pointers. You can also check out the code for this book, which has near 100% code coverage using mocha as the test runner.

To get the most out of this tip, you should know the basics of describe() and it() functions along with expectations.

Now, how do you write testable code? Here's a function that looks simple but has some subtle complexity.

functions/test/problem.js

```
Line 1  import { getTaxInformation } from './taxService';
     2
     3  function formatPrice(user, { price, location }) {
     4    const rate = getTaxInformation(location);
```

---

2. https://jasmine.github.io
3. https://mochajs.org
4. https://facebook.github.io/jest/

```
5    const taxes = rate ? `plus $${price * rate} in taxes.` : 'plus tax.';
6
7    return `${user} your total is: ${price} ${taxes}`;
8  }
9
10 export { formatPrice };
```

You may be wondering, how can this be complex? All it does is compute some tax information from a price and combines it with a user to create a string.

The testing difficulty begins when you call an outside function on line 4. Notice that you're importing that function at the top of the file. You'll learn more about importing functions in Tip 47, *Isolate Functionality with Import and Export*, on page 223, but for now, all you need to know is that you're getting something from outside the file.

The problem with using imported code directly is that the function is now tightly coupled with the imported function. You can't run formatPrice() without executing getTaxInformation(). And because the getTaxInformation() function will likely need to hit an external service or a config file, you're now tightly coupled to network communication. This means that if you run a test, the test will also have to access the API. Now your test is dependent on network access, response time, and so on. Again, this is a big problem. You're just trying to build a string.

To avoid the problem, you can create mocks that intercept imports and explicitly set a return value. Here's what a test would look like for the current function.

functions/test/problem.spec.js

```
Line 1  import expect from 'expect';
-
-       import sinon from 'sinon';
-       import * as taxService from './taxService';
5       import { formatPrice } from './problem';
-
-       describe('format price', () => {
-         let taxStub;
-
10        beforeEach(() => {
-           taxStub = sinon.stub(taxService, 'getTaxInformation');
-         });
-
-         afterEach(() => {
15          taxStub.restore();
-         });
-
-         it('should return plus tax if no tax info', () => {
-           taxStub.returns(null);
```

```
20      const item = { price: 30, location: 'Oklahoma' };
        const user = 'Aaron Cometbus';
        const message = formatPrice(user, item);
        const expectedMessage = 'Aaron Cometbus your total is: 30 plus tax.';
        expect(message).toEqual(expectedMessage);
25    });

      it('should return plus tax information', () => {
        taxStub.returns(0.1);

30      const item = { price: 30, location: 'Oklahoma' };
        const user = 'Aaron Cometbus';
        const message = formatPrice(user, item);
        const expectedMessage = 'Aaron Cometbus your total is:
                                 30 plus $3 in taxes.';
35      expect(message).toEqual(expectedMessage);
      });
    });
```

The tricky part begins on line 11. You're creating a stub that overrides the original getTaxInformation() function with a simple return value.

When you create a stub, you're bypassing the imported code and declaring what the output would be without running the actual code. The upside is that now you don't have to worry about any external dependencies. The downside is that you constantly have to set and reset the return value in every assertion. See line 19 for an example.

Finally, after the test suite is over, you have to restore the code to use the original method. You do this in the afterEach() method on line 15. Restoring the code is a crucial step. By hijacking the code in this test suite, you've hijacked it for *all* tests unless you restore it.

I once had a test suite that was tightly coupled and used a lot of stubs. Everything was working until I changed the location of a file. All of a sudden, the tests ran in a different order and lots of tests started failing. I thought I had accurately restored all the stubs, but it was an illusion. The only reason the test passed was because they ran in a specific order.

Don't be fooled by the shortness of the test suite. Tests that require a lot of external helpers, such as spies, mocks, and stubs, are a clue that your code is complex and may be tightly coupled. You should simplify your code.

Fortunately, the fix for tightly coupled code is fairly simple. You simply pass in your external functions as arguments. Passing in dependencies as arguments is called dependency injection.

Stubs, Mocks, Spies

Even with your best efforts, you'll eventually need some helpers to test your code. Fortunately there are quite a few techniques to help you. The three big ones are stubs, mocks, and spies.

In this example, you're working with stubs. You're overriding outside code and returning an explicit result. It's called a stub because you're removing all the underlying logic of the function and just declaring a result.

Mocks are a little more complex. They stand in for the objects they're replacing, and you make assertions based on the messages they'll receive and the methods you'll call on them. For example, you may mock an object and assert that you'll call a format() method on your object with the argument jabberwocky.

A crucial difference between mocks and stubs is that you set up the expectations before you call the code with mocks. Martin Fowler has a good article on the difference between mocks and stubs.[a]

Spies are like mocks, but you check how they were called after you execute the code. If you called formatPrice() and wanted to make sure that getTaxInformation() was called once with an argument of Iowa, you'd set up the stub with a spy and then, after calling formatPrice(), you'd make assertions on the spy. If you look at the code for this book, you'll see an occasional spy.

For more on mocks, spies, and stubs, Simon Coffey goes into detail on each, using Ruby as an example.[b]

---

a. https://martinfowler.com/articles/mocksArentStubs.html
b. https://about.futurelearn.com/blog/stubs-mocks-spies-rspec

To decouple your code, pass getTaxInformation() as an argument. You don't need to change anything else in your code.

functions/test/test.js
```js
function formatPrice(user, { price, location }, getTaxInformation) {
  const rate = getTaxInformation(location);
  const taxes = rate ? `plus $${price * rate} in taxes.` : 'plus tax.';
  return `${user} your total is: ${price} ${taxes}`;
}

export { formatPrice };
```

Now that you're using dependency injection, you don't need stubs. When you write your tests, you don't need to bypass an import. Instead, you pass a simple function that returns the value you want. It's a lot like stubbing but without any external dependencies. Your function now takes inputs, including another function, and returns outputs. Remember, you aren't testing getTaxInformation(). You're testing that formatPrice(), given certain inputs, will return a certain result.

Here's your test:

```
functions/test/test.spec.js
import expect from 'expect';

import { formatPrice } from './test';

describe('format price', () => {
  it('should return plus tax if no tax info', () => {
    const item = { price: 30, location: 'Oklahoma' };
    const user = 'Aaron Cometbus';
    const message = formatPrice(user, item, () => null);
    expect(message).toEqual('Aaron Cometbus your total is: 30 plus tax.');
  });

  it('should return plus tax information', () => {
    const item = { price: 30, location: 'Oklahoma' };
    const user = 'Aaron Cometbus';
    const message = formatPrice(user, item, () => 0.1);
    expect(message).toEqual('Aaron Cometbus your total is:
                            30 plus $3 in taxes.');
  });
});
```

Notice that you require nothing except the function you're testing and the expect library. The tests are much easier to write, and they do a better job of getting your code down to a single responsibility.

You may argue that dependency injection didn't solve the problem—it moved the problem to another function.

That's true. There are going to be some side effects, some input/output, in your code. The trick to writing testable code is to get that in as few places as possible.

For example, you can move all your AJAX calls into a service. Then, when you need to use them in a function, you can inject a service that's easy to test rather than trying to mock AJAX responses (which is very difficult).

The important thing to know is that there's a perception that writing tests is hard. That's just not true. If a test is hard to write, spend time rethinking your code. If your code isn't easy to test, you should change your code, not your tests.

And don't get frustrated when you encounter other problems. Tightly coupled code is just one form of complexity. There are plenty of other code smells—code that's technically correct but doesn't seem very clear— that sneak into tests. Joshua Mock wrote a good article on some of the other problems of testing JavaScript, and it's worth reading to learn more.[5]

The best thing you can do is start writing tests today. If you need more examples, check out the code for this book. It has nearly 100% test coverage and has a variety of tests (including some with mocks and spies). If you want to learn more, check out *Test Driving JavaScript Applications.* [Sub16]

In the next tip, we'll get back into the details of writing functions by further exploring arrow functions.

---

5.   https://www.toptal.com/javascript/writing-testable-code-in-javascript

Tip 33

Reduce Complexity with Arrow Functions

In this tip, you'll learn how to use arrow functions to destructure arguments, return objects, and construct higher-order functions.

You explored arrow functions once in Tip 20, *Simplify Looping with Arrow Functions*, on page 89. It's time to take a deeper dive.

As a reminder, arrow functions allow you to remove extraneous information, such as the function declaration, parentheses, return statements, even curly braces. Now you're going to see how to handle a few more concepts that you've just learned, such as destructuring. You'll also get an introduction to new ideas that you'll explore further in future tips.

Let's begin with destructuring. You're going to take an object that has a first and last name and combine them in a string. You can't get more simple than that.

```
functions/arrow/problem.js
const name = {
  first: 'Lemmy',
  last: 'Kilmister',
};

function getName({ first, last }) {
  return `${first} ${last}`;
}
```

That should be very easy to convert to an arrow function. Remove everything except the parameter and the template literal. Add a fat arrow, =>, and you should be done.

Not quite. Everything is the same except the parameters. When you're using any kind of special parameter action—destructuring, rest parameters, default parameters—you still need to include the parentheses.

This sounds trivial, but it will trip you up if you aren't aware. It's hard for the JavaScript engine to know if you're performing a function declaration and not an object declaration. You'll get an error like this:

```
functions/arrow/close.js
const getName = { first, last } => `${first} ${last}`;

// Error: Unexpected token '=>'. Expected ';' after variable declaration
```

And that's if you're lucky. If you try this in a Node.js REPL, it will just hang like you forgot to add a closing curly brace. It can be very confusing.

The solution is simple: If you're using any special parameters, just wrap the parameter in parentheses as you normally would.

functions/arrow/arrow.js
```
const comic = {
  first: 'Peter',
  last: 'Bagge',
  city: 'Seattle',
  state: 'Washington',
};

const getName = ({ first, last }) => `${first} ${last}`;
getName(comic);
// Peter Bagge
```

If you're returning an object, you have to be careful when omitting the return statement. Because an arrow function can't tell whether the curly braces are for an object or to wrap a function body, you'll need to indicate the return object by wrapping the whole thing in parentheses.

functions/arrow/arrow.js
```
const getFullName = ({ first, last }) => ({ fullName: `${first} ${last}` });
getFullName(comic);
// { fullName: 'Peter Bagge' }
```

It gets even better. When you return a value using parentheses, you aren't limited to a single line. You can return multi-line items while still omitting the return statement.

functions/arrow/arrow.js
```
const getNameAndLocation = ({ first, last, city, state }) => ({
  fullName: `${first} ${last}`,
  location: `${city}, ${state}`,
});
getNameAndLocation(comic);
// {
//    fullName: 'Peter Bagge',
//    location: 'Seattle, Washington'
// }
```

Finally, arrow functions are great ways to make higher-order functions—functions that return other functions. You'll explore higher-order functions in upcoming tips, so for now, let's just see how to structure them.

Because a higher-order function is merely a function that returns another function, the initial parameter is the same. And you can return a function from the body like you always would.

functions/arrow/problem.js
```
const discounter = discount => {
  return price => {
    return price * (1 - discount);
  };
};
const tenPercentOff = discounter(0.1);
tenPercentOff(100);
// 90
```

Of course, because the return value is another function, you can leverage the implicit return to return the function without even needing extra curly braces. Try it out.

functions/arrow/arrow.js
```
const discounter = discount => price => price * (1 - discount);

const tenPercentOff = discounter(0.1);
tenPercentOff(100);
// 90;
```

If you're anything like me, you're probably already forgetting all about higher-order functions. When are you going to use them? Turns out, they can be very helpful. Not only are they great ways to lock in parameters, but they'll also help you take some of the ideas you've already seen—array methods, rest parameters—even further.

In all the examples, you invoked the higher-order functions by first assigning the returned function to a variable before calling that with another parameter. That's not necessary. You can call one function after the other by just adding the second set of parameters in parentheses right after the first. This essentially turns a higher-order function into a single function with two different parameter sets.

functions/arrow/arrow.js
```
discounter(0.1)(100);
// 90
```

In the next tip, you'll see why using higher-order functions to keep parameters separate is such a game changer by learning how to create single responsibility parameters.

Tip 34

Maintain Single Responsibility Parameters with Partially Applied Functions

In this tip, you'll learn to keep parameters focused with partially applied functions.

In the last tip, you saw how you can easily create higher-order functions with arrow functions. If you come from an object-oriented background or just haven't seen much code that uses higher-order functions, you may have problems understanding when you should use higher-order functions.

Higher-order functions provide unique value by locking in parameters so you can complete the function later while still maintaining access to the original arguments. They also isolate parameters so you can keep intentions clear. In the next tip, you'll see more about locking in parameter data. In this tip, you'll see how you leverage higher-order functions to give parameters single responsibility.

A higher-order function is a function that returns another function. What this means is that you have at least two rounds of parameters before the function is fully resolved. With a partially applied function, you pass some parameters and you get back a function that locks those parameters in place while taking more parameters. In other words, a partially applied function reduces the total number of arguments for a function—also called the "arity"—while giving you another function that needs a few more arguments.

The takeaway is that you can have multiple sets of parameters that are independent of one another. Perhaps it seems like parameters already have single responsibility. They are, after all, the input data to the function so they must relate to one another. That's true, but even inputs have different relationships. Some inputs are related to one another while others are more independent.

Think about an events page on a website. An event is going to occur in a specific space. Each event is unique, but the space isn't going to change radically between events. The address, name, building hours, and so on will be the same. In addition, spaces are managed by people who are points of contact, and they will seldom change between events.

With that in mind, consider a function that needs to combine information about the space, the space manager, and an event on a page. You'll likely get each piece of information from a different source, and you'll need to combine them together to return the complete information.

Here's a sample of the data you'll receive. The building has an address and hours. The manager has a name and phone number. Then you have two different event types. The first, a program, will have a specific hour range that's shorter than the building hours. The second, an exhibit, will be open as long as the building is open but will need the curator as a contact.

```
functions/partial/partial.js
const building = {
  hours: '8 a.m. - 8 p.m.',
  address: 'Jayhawk Blvd',
};

const manager = {
  name: 'Augusto',
  phone: '555-555-5555',
};

const program = {
  name: 'Presenting Research',
  room: '415',
  hours: '3 - 6',
};

const exhibit = {
  name: 'Emerging Scholarship',
  contact: 'Dyan',
};
```

At this point, you just need to write a simple function that takes three arguments—building, manager, program/event—and combines them into one set of information.

```
functions/partial/problem.js
function mergeProgramInformation(building, manager, program) {
  const { hours, address } = building;
  const { name, phone } = manager;
  const defaults = {
    hours,
    address,
    contact: name,
    phone,
  };

  return { ...defaults, ...program };
}
```

Notice every time you call the function for a building, you have to pass the same first parameters. The function call is repetitive.

functions/partial/problem.js
```
const programInfo = mergeProgramInformation(building, manager, program);

const exhibitInfo = mergeProgramInformation(building, manager, exhibit);
```

This repetition is a clue that your function has a natural division. The first two parameters are establishing a base for a building, which is then applied to a series of programs and exhibits.

A higher-order function can create single responsibility parameters, allowing you to reuse the first two arguments. The responsibility of the first set of parameters is to gather baseline data. The second set will be the custom information that overrides the baseline.

To accomplish this, you need to make the top function take only two parameters—the building and the manager—and have it return a function that takes only one parameter—a program (which could be a program, an event, an exhibit, and so on).

functions/partial/partial.js
```
function mergeProgramInformation(building, manager) {
  const { hours, address } = building;
  const { name, phone } = manager;
  const defaults = {
    hours,
    address,
    contact: name,
    phone,
  };

  return program => {
    return { ...defaults, ...program };
  };
}
```

This can look intimidating, but it's actually simple. Again, a higher-order function is just a function that needs to be called multiple time before it's fully resolved. That's all. To invoke both parts of the functions in a single call, all you have to do is put parentheses right after one another. This invokes the outer function, then immediately invokes the inner function. The result is the same as before.

functions/partial/partial.js
```
const programInfo = mergeProgramInformation(building, manager)(program);
// {
//    name: 'Presenting Research',
//    room: '415',
```

```
//    hours: '3 - 6',
//    address: 'Jayhawk Blvd',
//    contact: 'Augusto',
//    phone: '555-555-5555'
// }
const exhibitInfo = mergeProgramInformation(building, manager)(exhibit);
// {
//    name: 'Emerging Scholarship',
//    contact: 'Dyan'
//    hours: '8 a.m. - 8 p.m.',
//    address: 'Jayhawk Blvd'
//    phone: '555-555-5555'
// }
```

You may have given the parameters a single responsibility, but it doesn't eliminate the repetition. Fortunately, with partial application, you can get around that problem also. You'll see how you can reuse a returned function in the next tip.

To finish up, there's another reason to use partial application and higher-order functions to give your parameters single responsibility: you can reuse the rest operator.

As you probably remember from Tip 31, *Pass a Variable Number of Arguments with the Rest Operator*, on page 143, nothing can come after the rest parameter. In other words, you can only have a single rest parameter in a set of arguments. That's fine most of the time, but occasionally you'll have a situation where you want to have multiple rest parameters.

This comes up often when you have an array of data and more data that has a one-to-one correspondence with your original data.

For example, if you have a function that takes an array of states and returns the state bird, the resulting array is nice, but you'll eventually need to connect the original and the result together into a nice array of pairs.

functions/partial/partial.js
```
const birds = getBirds('kansas', 'wisconsin', 'new mexico');
// ['meadowlark', 'robin', 'roadrunner']
```

Combining two arrays into pairs is so common that it has a name: "zip."

To write a zip function that can take multiple parameters, you need to write a higher-order function that takes the original array (call it left), returns a function that takes the results array (right), and combines them. Guess what? Because the parameters are independent, you can use your rest parameters both times.

functions/partial/partial.js
```
const zip = (...left) => (...right) => {
  return left.map((item, i) => [item, right[i]]);
};
zip('kansas', 'wisconsin', 'new mexico')(...birds);
// [
//   ['kansas', 'meadowlark'],
//   ['wisconsin', 'robin'],
//   ['new mexico', 'roadrunner']
// ]
```

This isn't a technique you'll use often, but it's very valuable when you want to keep an interface clear. Sometimes parameters just don't belong together, yet you still need all the information. Partially applied functions are a great way to combine parameters without a lot of effort.

In the next tip, you'll go even further and learn how you can invoke a function once to capture information and then reuse it over and over again.

Tip 35

Combine Currying and Array Methods for Partial Application

In this tip, you'll learn to lock in variables with partial application of functions.

In the previous tip, you saw how you can give parameters a single responsibility with higher-order functions and partial application. It solved the problem of having unrelated parameters, but it didn't solve the problem of using the same parameters over and over. You still passed in the same parameters multiple times.

With higher-order functions, you can avoid repetition by creating a new function with values you lock in once and use later. When you return a higher-order function, you don't have to invoke it right away. After you invoke it once, you have another pre-made function that you can use over and over. It's like you wrote it with the argument hard-coded.

To reuse the building and manager from the previous tip, you can assign the return value from the first function call to a variable. You now have a pre-built function with some information locked in place.

Invoking it once and reusing the captured parameters is no different from declaring a function knowing the inside variables ahead of time. These are equivalent.

functions/partial/program.js
```
const setStrongHallProgram = mergeProgramInformation(building, manager);

const programInfo = setStrongHallProgram(program);

const exhibitInfo = setStrongHallProgram(exhibit);
```

functions/curry/higherorder.js
```
const setStrongHallProgram = program => {
  const defaults = {
    hours: '8 a.m. - 8 p.m.',
    address: 'Jayhawk Blvd',
    name: 'Augusto',
    phone: '555-555-5555'
  }
  return { ...defaults, ...program}
}

const programs = setStrongHallProgram(program);

const exhibit = setStrongHallProgram(exhibit);
```

You built the first function with partial application of a higher-order function. You built the second function with hard-coded information. A higher-order function that takes two rounds of arguments will be more flexible than the one with hard-coded information, but it helps to think about how they're similar.

You know higher-order functions can keep parameters separate, but they have an even more important use: separating arguments so that you can reduce the number of arguments that a function needs before it's fully resolved. Building functions that take only one argument at a time is called "currying," and it's an invaluable technique when you're working with methods that pass only one argument. And although currying in its pure form isn't fully supported in JavaScript,[6] partially applying a function to reduce parameters to a series of single parameters is common.

Currying and Partial Application

Partially applied functions can take multiple rounds of parameters. This is often confused with currying. And it's true that currying and partial application are very similar, but they're different.

Partially applied functions and curried functions both reduce the number of arguments by returning functions that need fewer arguments than the original. The total number of arguments for a function to fully resolve is called the arity. A partially applied function returns a function that has a smaller arity than the original function. If you need three total arguments and you pass two, the returned function will need only one argument. The original function had a total arity of three. With partial application, you returned a function with an arity of one.

Currying, by contrast, is when you take a function that would require multiple arguments and return a series of functions that take *exactly* one argument. If you had a function that requires three arguments to resolve, you'd need a higher-order function that takes one argument and returns a function that takes one argument, which returns a function that takes one argument that finally resolves.

Think back to when you were filtering an array of dogs in Tip 22, *Create Arrays of a Similar Size with map()*, on page 98. At that point, you only added the filters—you never applied them. Here's a slightly modified version of your array of dogs.

functions/curry/curry.js
```
const dogs = [
  {
    name: 'max',
    weight: 10,
```

_____

6. http://2ality.com/2017/11/currying-in-js.html

```
    breed: 'boston terrier',
    state: 'wisconsin',
    color: 'black',
  },
  {
    name: 'don',
    weight: 90,
    breed: 'labrador',
    state: 'kansas',
    color: 'black',
  },
  {
    name: 'shadow',
    weight: 40,
    breed: 'labrador',
    state: 'wisconsin',
    color: 'chocolate',
  },
];
```

Try to write a function that takes the dogs and a filter and returns just the names of the dogs that match the filter.

Pass the dogs as the first parameter and use a combination of array methods—filter() and map()—to get the final result set.

functions/curry/problem.js
```
function getDogNames(dogs, filter) {
  const [key, value] = filter;
  return dogs
    .filter(dog => dog[key] === value)
    .map(dog => dog.name);
}

getDogNames(dogs, ['color', 'black']);
// ['max', 'don']
```

This function looks pretty good, but it's actually severely limited. There are two issues.

First, your filter function is constrained. It will work only when you're doing an exact comparison between a filter and each individual dog. In other words, it works only when using ===. What if you need to do a different comparison, such as finding all the dogs below a certain weight?

Second, the map, like all array methods, can take only one argument—the item being checked—so you have to somehow get your other variables in scope. Because map is a function inside another function, it has access to the variables in the wrapper function. That means you'll need to figure out how to pass them in as parameters to the outside function.

Start by trying to solve the first problem. Rewrite the function so that you can find all dogs below a certain weight. As you saw in Tip 32, *Write Functions for Testability*, on page 151, you can inject functions into other functions. Start there. Instead of hard coding a comparison function, pass in the filter function as a callback.

functions/curry/curry.js

```
function getDogNames(dogs, filterFunc) {
  return dogs
  .filter(filterFunc)
  .map(dog => dog.name)
}

getDogNames(dogs, dog => dog.weight < 20);
// ['max']
```

You're partway there, but you're still forced to hard code a value, the number 20 in this case. This means you'll still have to either code the value by hand or make sure there are no scope conflicts if you're using a variable. This may not seem like a big deal, but scope conflicts creep in when you least expect them. It's much better to inject values in a function rather than trust them to be able to access variables in an upper scope at runtime.

The goal is to have a partially applied function with some values locked in. You can assign a partially applied function to a variable and pass it as data to another function, which can then provide the remaining arguments.

At this point, you don't even need to rewrite your getDogNames() function. It takes any comparison function, so you're all set. What you do need to do is rewrite your comparison function so that you don't need to hard code the comparison value.

Use the technique from the previous tip to create two sets of arguments—the first argument will be a weight, the second set will be the individual dog.

Now you can apply the function first with one weight and another time with a different weight. The actual number will be locked in the function. This means you can reuse the function over and over with different weights. Scope conflicts will be much less likely.

functions/curry/curry.js

```
const weightCheck = weight => dog => dog.weight < weight;

getDogNames(dogs, weightCheck(20));
// ['max']

getDogNames(dogs, weightCheck(50));
// ['max', 'shadow']
```

By currying the function, you've made it so you can pass multiple parameters at different points. You're also able to pass a function around as data.

And the best part is you don't need to limit yourself to just two functions and two sets of arguments. What if you wanted to rewrite your original comparison function using currying?

First, you'd pass in the field you want to compare, such as color. In the next function, you'd pass the value you want to compare against, such as black. The final function takes the individual dog.

The result is a set of comparisons you build up using the same logic but different parameters.

```
functions/curry/curry.js
const identity = field => value => dog => dog[field] === value;
const colorCheck = identity('color');
const stateCheck = identity('state');

getDogNames(dogs, colorCheck('chocolate'));
// ['shadow']

getDogNames(dogs, stateCheck('kansas'));
// ['don']
```

Now think about what you've created. You took a function that had specific requirements and made something abstract that can take many different comparisons. Because you can assign partially applied functions to variables, they're now just another piece of data you can pass around. This means you can build very sophisticated comparisons using a small set of simple tools.

For example, if you only wanted dogs that meet every criteria, you can pass an array of checks and use the every() array method, which returns true if *all* values return true.

If you only wanted the dogs that meet at least one criteria, you can write a function that uses the some() array method, which returns true if *any* value returns true.

```
functions/curry/curry.js
function allFilters(dogs, ...checks) {
  return dogs
  .filter(dog => checks.every(check => check(dog)))
  .map(dog => dog.name);
}
allFilters(dogs, colorCheck('black'), stateCheck('kansas'));
// ['Don']
```

```
function anyFilters(dogs, ...checks) {
  return dogs
  .filter(dog => checks.some(check => check(dog)))
  .map(dog => dog.name);
}
anyFilters(dogs, weightCheck(20), colorCheck('chocolate'));
// ['max', 'shadow']
```

Does that make your head spin? Hopefully not. Copy the code into a REPL and try playing with it. That's the best way to learn. Just remember this: If you have functions that can't take more than one argument, currying is a great tool. It makes otherwise complicated problems very straightforward.

In the next tip, you'll see a problem related to variable scope—context. You'll learn how to use arrow functions to solve nagging problems related to the this keyword.

Tip 36

Prevent Context Confusion with Arrow Functions

In this tip, you'll learn how to use the arrow function to avoid context errors.

Scope and context are probably the two most confusing concepts for JavaScript developers. A function's scope, at it simplest, is what variables the functions can access. We explored this previously in Tip 3, *Isolate Information with Block Scoped Variables*, on page 10. Now you're going to learn about context. Context is what the keyword this refers to in a function or class.

Not only are both concepts hard to grasp, but people often confuse them. I know I confuse them all the time. Ryan Morr gives a simple way to remember the difference: Scope pertains to functions and context pertains to objects.[7] While that's not 100 percent true—you can use this in any function—it's a good general rule.

To understand context, start with a very simple object. For example, think about an object called Validator, which sets an invalid message on form fields. You have one property, message, and one method, setInvalidMessage().

In the setInvalidMessage() method, you can refer to the message property using this.message. To see it in action, call the method from the object.

```
functions/context/basic.js
const validator = {
  message: 'is invalid.',
  setInvalidMessage(field) {
    return `${field} ${this.message}`;
  },
};

validator.setInvalidMessage('city');
// city is invalid.
```

As you see, this.message refers to the property on the object. This works because, when the method is called from the object, the function creates a this binding with the containing object as context.

Now before you go any further, you should know that concepts surrounding the keyword this are pretty complex. There's a whole book in the *You Don't*

---

7. http://ryanmorr.com/understanding-scope-and-context-in-javascript/

Know JS [Sim14] series on the subject. This book is mandatory reading for JavaScript developers, and there's no way to cover the same level of information here in one tip. Instead, you're going to see one of the most common context mistakes.

Working with this on objects usually isn't a problem until you try to use a function as callback for another function.

For example, you'll encounter problems with this when using setTimeout(), setInterval(), or your favorite array methods such as map() or filter(). Each of these functions takes a callback, which, as you'll see, changes the context of the callback.

What do you think will happen if you try to refactor your setInvalidMessage() method to take an array of fields using map() to add the message? The code change isn't complicated. Create a new method called setInvalidMessages() that maps over an array adding the message to each.

```
functions/context/problem.js
const validator = {
  message: 'is invalid.',
  setInvalidMessages(...fields) {
    return fields.map(function (field) {
      return `${field} ${this.message}`;
    });
  },
};
```

The problem is that when you invoke the function, you'll get either a TypeError or undefined. This is where most developers get frustrated and refactor the code to remove a reference to this.

```
functions/context/context.spec.js
validatorProblem.setInvalidMessages(field);
// TypeError: Cannot read property 'message' of undefined
```

Think for a moment about what may cause this problem. Remember that whenever you call a function, it creates a this binding based on where it's called. setInvalidMessage() was called in the context of an object. The this context was the object. The callback for the map function is called in the context of the map() method, so the this binding is no longer the Validator object. It will actually be the global object: window in a browser and the Node.js environment in a REPL. The callback doesn't have access to the message property.

This is where arrow functions come in. Arrow functions don't create a new this binding when you use them. If you were to rewrite the preceding map() callback using an arrow function, everything would work as expected.

```
functions/context/context.js
const validator = {
  message: 'is invalid.',
  setInvalidMessages(...fields) {
    return fields.map(field => {
      return `${field} ${this.message}`;
    });
  },
};

validator.setInvalidMessages('city');
// ['city is invalid.]
```

Now this may seem great and a good reason to always use arrow functions. But remember, sometimes you actually do want to set a this context.

For example, what if you wrote your original setInvalidMessage() method not as a named method but as an arrow function assigned to a property?

```
functions/context/method.js
const validator = {
  message: 'is invalid.',
  setInvalidMessage: field => `${field} ${this.message}`,
};
```

You'd have the exact same TypeError when you called it.

```
functions/context/context.spec.js
validatorMethod.setInvalidMessage(field);
// TypeError: Cannot read property 'message' of undefined
```

In this case, you didn't create a new this context binding to the current object. Because you didn't create a new context, you're still bound to the global object.

To summarize, arrow functions are great when you already have a context and want to use the function inside another function. They're a problem when you need to set a new this binding.

This isn't the last you'll see of this. It plays a big part in classes, and context bindings will come up again in Tip 42, *Resolve Context Problems with Bind()*, on page 198.

The next chapter explores classes in JavaScript. If you come from an object-oriented background, you'll see a lot that looks familiar and a lot that you won't expect.

CHAPTER 8

Keep Interfaces Clear with Classes

An octopus has a brain. But in a way, it has many brains. Neurons run throughout an octopus's body, so in a sense, it can think with its arms. If its arm is removed from its body, it can still respond to stimulus, change color, and reach and grab for items.

This poses a challenge to researchers. An octopus can think, but not in the way mammals do. It responds similarly—it can remember specific people, prefer certain types of food, and even plan an escape—but the way its consciousness works is unusual. An octopus's mind is similar but different.

In this chapter, we're going to explore concepts that are familiar, but they're also different. Developers have been complaining for years about these differences—they say JavaScript is broken because it doesn't behave like other object-oriented languages. The problem isn't that it's different. It's that it's just similar enough to create confusion.

In ES6+, things have gotten even more confusing because now JavaScript uses familiar syntax—class, extend,static—but the code doesn't always act as you'd expect if you come from another object-oriented language. In this chapter, you're going to recognize how classes in JavaScript are different even while they use many familiar concepts.

To start off, you'll build and extend a class. This will look similar to most object-oriented languages. After that, you'll see how classes work under the hood by combining class syntax and JavaScript prototypes. Next, you'll learn how to mask complexity with getters, setters, and generators. Finally, you will return to common problems with the this keyword and techniques for solving them.

Remember that classes in JavaScript are a little different, but they still retain many of the benefits—and some of the problems—of class syntax. Classes will help you organize your code, build new instances of objects, and store local properties. Just keep in mind that JavaScript is its own language with a unique history and paradigm. Learn how you can use classes to fuse your existing knowledge of both JavaScript and other object-oriented languages.

Tip 37

Build Readable Classes

In this tip, you'll learn how to create extendable classes in JavaScript.

One of the longest running criticisms of JavaScript was that it lacked a class syntax. Well it's here! But it didn't arrive without controversy. Proponents of classes argue it's a common development paradigm that's very familiar to developers in other languages. Skeptics think it obscures the underlying nature of the language and encourages bad habits.

Like many controversies, the rhetoric is excessive. Classes are now part of JavaScript, and if you use any popular framework such as Angular or React, you'll introduce them in your code. And that's great.

As you'll see in Tip 39, *Extend Existing Prototypes with Class*, on page 184, the base language hasn't changed. JavaScript is still a prototype-based language. Now you have familiar syntax masking slightly complicated concepts. As a result, there are some surprises.

In this tip, you'll get a quick look at how to write classes in JavaScript. If you've written classes in any other language, the interface should seem pretty familiar.

To start off, make a class called Coupon. You declare a class with the class keyword. You can then create new instances using the new keyword.

classes/constructor/problem.js
```
class Coupon {

}

const coupon = new Coupon();
```

When you create an instance of a class, the first thing you're doing is running a constructor function, which can define a number of properties. You aren't forced to declare a constructor function, but it's where you will declare your properties, so you'll write one in most cases.

The next step is to create a constructor method. You'll need to name it constructor(). Add it to the class using what looks like function syntax, but without the function keyword. Because the constructor is a function, you can pass as many arguments as you want.

Part of the job of the constructor is creating a this context. Inside your constructor, you add properties to a class by assigning them to this with a key like you would if you were adding key-values to an object. And because you're able to pass arguments to the constructor, you can dynamically set properties when you create a new instance. Currently, you are required to set all properties inside the constructor. That will likely change in the future.

For now, set two properties on your Coupon: price and expiration. After setting the properties, you can call them using the familiar dot syntax or even array syntax. Remember that this is still JavaScript, and you're still working with objects.

```
classes/constructor/constructor.js
class Coupon {
  constructor(price, expiration) {
    this.price = price;
    this.expiration = expiration || 'two weeks';
  }
}

const coupon = new Coupon(5);
coupon.price;
// 5
coupon['expiration'];
// 'Two Weeks'
```

Note that you aren't declaring properties as public or private. Currently, everything is public. Private fields—properties or methods—are working their way through the TC39 committee.

The class and object instance are getting a little more interesting, but they still can't do much. The next step is to add two simple methods: getPriceText() to return a formatted price and getExpirationMessage() to get a formatted message.

You can add methods using the same syntax as a constructor. The methods will be normal functions, not arrow functions. This may not seem like a big deal, but arrow functions behave differently in classes than normal functions, just as you saw in Tip 36, *Prevent Context Confusion with Arrow Functions*, on page 171. You'll see how to use arrow functions in classes in Tip 42, *Resolve Context Problems with Bind()*, on page 198.

Speaking of context. You have full access to the this context in the methods if you call them directly on an instance of a class. This will work as predicted most of the time. You'll see the exceptions in upcoming tips.

This means that you can create methods that refer to properties or other methods.

classes/constructor/methods.js

```
class Coupon {
  constructor(price, expiration) {
    this.price = price;
    this.expiration = expiration || 'two weeks';
  }

  getPriceText() {
    return `$ ${this.price}`;
  }

  getExpirationMessage() {
    return `This offer expires in ${this.expiration}.`;
  }
}

const coupon = new Coupon(5);
coupon.getPriceText();
// '$ 5'
coupon.getExpirationMessage();
// 'This offer expires in two weeks.'
```

Now that you have a very basic but useful class, you can create a new object using a constructor function that sets up a this binding. You can call methods and access properties. And everything uses an intuitive interface. The basics are familiar, but it's important you note the quirks, particularly in regard to setting properties. You're building objects, so you'll still encounter some context and scope issues.

In the next tip, you'll see how to share code between classes using inheritance.

Tip 38

Share Methods with Inheritance

In this tip, you'll learn how to extend classes and call parent methods.

In the previous tip, you learned how to create basic classes with properties and methods. You may recall that classes in JavaScript were highly anticipated and slightly dreaded. The core of the controversy is inheritance.

Inheriting methods on prototypes was a pretty complex process in early versions of JavaScript. First, you had to loop through the properties on an object; then, you had to check to see that each property existed specifically on an object as a property and not on the object prototype. Then you had to copy the prototype from the parent to a new object before adding further methods.

It was hard.

With classes, inheritance is easy. Still, in recent years, JavaScript developers have soured on inheritance. They argue that too much inheritance is a bad thing and that it leads to bloated code. There are other techniques for sharing methods that don't require inheritance (such as composition). In other words, use inheritance with caution.

How does inheritance work? Return to your Coupon class. Suppose you want a FlashCoupon that has deeper discounts but a shorter time span. To create that class, simply declare a new class called FlashCoupon that inherits from the Coupon class using the extends keyword.

Your new FlashCoupon class inherits all the existing properties and methods. For example, you can access the price and the getPriceText() method.

classes/extend/basic.js
```
import Coupon from './extend';

class FlashCoupon extends Coupon {

}

const flash = new FlashCoupon(10);

flash.price;
// 10

flash.getPriceText();
// "$ 10"
```

Of course, there's really no point in inheriting code if you aren't going to add new properties or methods. To make this coupon different, add a new default expiration. Make the new default expiration "two hours" instead of "two weeks."

To make the change, set up a constructor function that takes price and expiration, as you did on the parent. In this constructor, you'll need to call super() to access the parent constructor. super() calls the parent constructor, so pass through any arguments the parent constructor might need. In this case, you'll need to pass the price to the parent constructor. After that, you can set any new properties or override any properties that the parent constructor might set.

For the FlashCoupon, you're setting the expiration, but you don't need to worry about setting the price. The parent constructor takes care of that.

classes/extend/constructor.js
```
import Coupon from './extend';

class FlashCoupon extends Coupon {
  constructor(price, expiration) {
    super(price);
    this.expiration = expiration || 'two hours';
  }
}
const flash = new FlashCoupon(10);

flash.price;
// 10

flash.getExpirationMessage();
// "This offer expires in two hours"
```

You're using the parent getExpirationMessage() method, but you're using the child's expiration property. When you call getExpirationMessage(), you'll see the familiar message with the new default expiration.

Of course, you may not like that message. This is a flash coupon after all. You should alert your users that this coupon is special. Any time you call a method, the JavaScript engine first checks to see if the method exists on the current class. If not, the engine goes up the chain, checking each class or prototype along the way. This means you can override any method by creating a new method with the same name.

Try adding a new method called getExpirationMessage() to the FlashCoupon class. This method will be the same as the parent method except that it returns a message of This is a flash offer and expires in ${this.expiration}.

At this point, you've created a class that inherits methods and properties. You called the parent constructor to set some properties and overrode other properties. You also wrote methods that override parent methods.

The last step is to write methods that invoke the parent methods. To start, add two new methods to your Coupon class. First, add the method getRewards(), which takes a user and then calls isRewardsEligible() to find out if the user is eligible for further discounts. If the user is eligible for further discounts, reduce the price.

As a warning, any method you add to a parent class is inherited by a child class. This can be a huge benefit, but it's also easy to create bloat in child classes by adding methods to parents that aren't necessary in child classes.

```
classes/extend/extend.js
class Coupon {
  constructor(price, expiration) {
    this.price = price;
    this.expiration = expiration || 'Two Weeks';
  }

  getPriceText() {
    return `$ ${this.price}`;
  }

  getExpirationMessage() {
    return `This offer expires in ${this.expiration}`;
  }

  isRewardsEligible(user) {
    return user.rewardsEligible && user.active;
  }

  getRewards(user) {
    if (this.isRewardsEligible(user)) {
      this.price = this.price * 0.9;
    }
  }
}

export default Coupon;
```

Giving users a discount is great, but because flash coupons are an even bigger savings, you'll probably want to give eligible users a larger discount on flash coupons. But you don't want to give away too much. Instead, you only want to give your eligible users a discount if the previous conditions are met, a user is active and is rewards-eligible, and the base price of the item is $20 or more.

To add this in, first create a method of the same name in the FlashCoupon class. Then, in the isRewardsEligible() method, first call the parent method by calling the method name on super(). After that, add your additional code. Note that super() in the constructor doesn't need a specific method call, but if you want to call any other methods on the parent class, you'll have to specify them, even when they're in a method of the same name.

The result is a class that inherits some properties and functions from a parent while overriding others.

```
classes/extend/flash.js
import Coupon from './extend';

class FlashCoupon extends Coupon {
  constructor(price, expiration) {
    super(price);
    this.expiration = expiration || 'two hours';
  }
  getExpirationMessage() {
    return `This is a flash offer and expires in ${this.expiration}.`;
  }
  isRewardsEligible(user) {
    return super.isRewardsEligible(user) && this.price > 20;
  }
  getRewards(user) {
    if (this.isRewardsEligible(user)) {
      this.price = this.price * 0.8;
    }
  }
}

export { FlashCoupon };
```

That's all there is to it. For those familiar with object-oriented programming, this should be very familiar. Still, you should remember that JavaScript isn't the same as Ruby, Java, or other languages that use classes. JavaScript is a prototype language. Classes as you're using them are simply a familiar syntax for a different paradigm. The benefit is that because they are using the same prototype actions under the hood, you can combine classes with legacy code.

In the next tip, you'll see how classes relate to pre-ES6 JavaScript and how you can combine the two approaches in the same codebase.

| Tip 39 |

Extend Existing Prototypes with Class

In this tip, you'll learn how to use classes with existing prototypes.

Now that you know how to write classes in JavaScript, it's time to see how the new class syntax relates to JavaScript prototypes. It's important to understand that classes in JavaScript and prototypes aren't different. Classes are just a clean way to write regular JavaScript. By understanding how classes in JavaScript differ from traditional object-oriented languages, you'll be able to integrate new syntax with legacy code and prevent subtle bugs from surfacing.

What are the differences between JavaScript and more traditional object-oriented languages? Here are the basics: When you use a class in traditional object-oriented languages, such as Ruby, it's a blueprint for an object. When you create a new instance, you copy all the properties and methods onto the new object.[1]

JavaScript is a prototype language. When you create a new instance, you aren't copying methods. You're creating a link to a prototype. When you call a method on an instance of an object, you're calling it from the prototype, which is itself an object instance (not a blueprint). Eric Elliot has a longer article on the subject.[2]

When you see the word class in JavaScript, you should know that it isn't new functionality. It's just a shorthand for a prototype. That means you can integrate class syntax with your current code bases.

Up to this point, you've created object instances from classes, but not from constructor functions. In pre-ES5 JavaScript, when you wanted to create a new object instance using the new keyword, you'd use a function. You'll notice that constructor functions are very similar to a constructor method on a class. That should be a clue that new syntax will fit in nicely with legacy code.

To make an object instance with a constructor function in JavaScript, you'd simply write a function as normal. By convention, when you intend to use a

---

1. https://github.com/getify/You-Dont-Know-JS/blob/master/this%20%26%20object%20prototypes/ch4.md
2. https://medium.com/javascript-scene/master-the-javascript-interview-what-s-the-difference-between-class-prototypal-inheritance-e4cd0a7562e9

function as a constructor, you'd start the function with a capital letter. Inside the function, you can attach properties to an instance using the this keyword.

When you create a new instance using the new keyword, you run the function as a constructor and bind the this context. Here's Coupon written as a constructor function.

classes/prototypes/prototypes.js
```
function Coupon(price, expiration) {
  this.price = price;
  this.expiration = expiration || 'two weeks';
}
const coupon = new Coupon(5, 'two months');
coupon.price;
// 5
```

That should look familiar. All you did is pull out your constructor function into a standalone action. The only problem is you lost all your methods. This is precisely where JavaScript diverges from traditional object-oriented languages.

When you created a new instance with new, you ran the constructor and bound a this context, but you didn't copy methods. You can add methods to this in the constructor, but it's far more efficient to add directly to a prototype.

A prototype is an object that's the base for the constructor function. All object instances derive properties from the prototype. In addition, new instances can also use methods on the prototype.

To add a method to a prototype, you use the constructor name, Coupon, and you add the method to the prototype property as if you were adding a function or property to an object instance. Add the getExpirationMessage() method to the prototype. Now remember, you already have a working instance of Coupon. Because you're working with an instance of a prototype, you can access a method you add even after you've created a new instance.

classes/prototypes/prototypes.js
```
Coupon.prototype.getExpirationMessage = function () {
  return `This offer expires in ${this.expiration}.`;
};
coupon.getExpirationMessage();
// This offer expires in two months.
```

When you create an object using the class keyword, you're still creating prototypes and binding contexts, but with a more intuitive interface.

The code you just created using constructor functions and prototypes is identical to the classes you created in previous tips. It looks different, but behind the scenes, you're still creating a prototype.

And because they're the same, you can write classes for legacy code that you built using prototypes. For example, if you wanted to extend the Coupon prototype, the process would be the exact same as when you extended the Coupon you built with class syntax. You merely declare that you're extending the Coupon prototype when you create your new class.

classes/prototypes/prototypes.js
```
class FlashCoupon extends Coupon {
  constructor(price, expiration) {
    super(price);
    this.expiration = expiration || 'two hours';
  }

  getExpirationMessage() {
    return `This is a flash offer and expires in ${this.expiration}.`;
  }
}
```

If you spend lots of time with JavaScript, it's worth exploring other ideas such as the prototypal chain, but for now, all you need to know is that classes aren't new functionality. It's just a new name for an old concept. Check out the Mozilla Developer Network for a few more examples of how classes relate to prototypes.[3]

In the next tip, you'll return to class syntax and explore how to make simple interfaces using get and set.

---

3. https://developer.mozilla.org/en-US/docs/Web/JavaScript/Reference/Classes#Sub_classing_with_extends

Tip 40

Simplify Interfaces with get and set

In this tip, you'll learn how to mask logic behind simple interfaces with get and set.

You have the basics of classes. You can create instances, call properties, call methods, and extend parent classes. But it won't be long before someone tries to alter a property you had no intention of exposing. Or maybe someone sets the wrong data type on a property, creating bugs because the code expects an integer, not a string.

One of the major problems in JavaScript is that there are no private properties by default. Everything is exposed. You can't control what the users of your class do with the methods or properties.

Think about your Coupon. It has a property of price, which you initially set in the constructor. A user of the class can access the property on an instance with dot syntax: coupon.price. So far, no problem. But because an instance of Coupon is just an object, the user can also change the property: coupon.price = 11.

In itself that's not a big deal. But you'll eventually hit a problem where another developer (or, admit it, you yourself) innocently tries to set a value other parts of the code may not expect. For example, what if instead of setting the price with an integer, you set it using a string? The change may seem harmless, but because all methods expect an integer, the change could ripple through the class, creating unexpected bugs.

classes/get/problem.js
```js
class Coupon {
  constructor(price, expiration) {
    this.price = price;
    this.expiration = expiration || 'Two Weeks';
  }
  getPriceText() {
    return `$ ${this.price}`;
  }
  getExpirationMessage() {
    return `This offer expires in ${this.expiration}`;
  }
}
```

```
const coupon = new Coupon(5);
coupon.price = '$10';
coupon.getPriceText();
// '$ $10'
```

When you set the price to a string, your message looks broken. What can you do about it?

One solution is to put properties behind extra logic using getters and setters. A getter or setter is a way to mask complexity by making a function appear like a property.

The change is very simple. You already have a few functions that are clearly getting data. You have a getPriceText() method and a getExpirationMessage() method that have the word "get" built right in the function name. And, of course, to execute the method, you call it with dot syntax: coupon.getPriceText().

Refactoring the method to a getter is simple. You simply add the keyword get in front of the method. After that, you can also rename the function to be a noun instead of an action. By convention, methods or functions are usually verbs and properties are usually nouns.

Here are your methods converted to getters. Notice the only change is the get keyword.

classes/get/price.js

```
class Coupon {
  constructor(price, expiration) {
    this.price = price;
    this.expiration = expiration || 'two weeks';
  }

  get priceText() {
    return `$ ${this.price}`;
  }

  get expirationMessage() {
    return `This offer expires in ${this.expiration}.`;
  }
}
```

After making that small change, you can call the method using dot syntax but without the parentheses. The method acts like a property even though you're executing code.

classes/get/price.js

```
const coupon = new Coupon(5);
coupon.price = 10;
coupon.priceText;
// '$10'
```

```
coupon.messageText;
// 'This offer expires in two weeks.
coupon.messageText;
```

This makes information easier to retrieve, but it doesn't solve your problem of someone setting a bad value. To address that, you also need to create a setter.

A setter works like your getter. It masks a method by making the method appear like a property. A setter, though, accepts a single argument and changes a property rather than just exposing information. You don't pass the argument using parentheses. Instead, you pass the object using the equal sign (=) as if you were setting a value on an object.

As an example, make a setter that sets the price to half of an argument. This may not be a very useful setter, but it will show you how easy it is to mask method logic behind a setter.

To create a setter, you add the keyword set in front of a method. Inside the method, you can change a value on a property.

classes/get/set.js
```
class Coupon {
  constructor(price, expiration) {
    this.price = price;
    this.expiration = expiration || 'Two Weeks';
  }

  set halfPrice(price) {
    this.price = price / 2;
  }
}
```

The problem with setters is that if you don't have a corresponding getter, things get a little odd. You can set a value to halfPrice. It looks like it's a normal property, but you can't get a value from halfPrice.

classes/get/set.js
```
const coupon = new Coupon(5);
coupon.price;
// 5
coupon.halfPrice = 20;
coupon.price;
// 10
coupon.halfPrice;
// undefined
```

For this reason, it's always a good idea to pair getters and setters. In fact, they can (and should) have the same name. That's perfectly valid. What you can't do is have a property with the same name as your getter or setter. That would be invalid and create a lot of confusion.

For example, if you tried to make a setter of price, it would trigger an infinite call stack.

classes/get/invalid.js
```
class Coupon {
  constructor(price, expiration) {
    this.price = price;
    this.expiration = expiration || 'Two Weeks';
  }

  get price() {
    return this.price;
  }

  set price(price) {
    this.price = `$ ${price}`;
  }
}

const coupon = new Coupon(5);
// RangeError: Maximum call stack size exceeded
```

The solution is to use another property as a bridge between your getter and setter. You don't want users or other developers to access your bridge property. You want it to be for internal use only. In most languages, you'd use a private property. Because you don't have those currently in JavaScript, you must rely on convention.

Developers signal that a method or property is private by prepending it with an underscore. If you see an object with a property of _price, you should know you shouldn't access it directly.

After you set an intermediate property, you can use getters and setters with the same name, minus the underscore, to access or update the value.

You now have the tools to solve your problem with setting a non-integer to price. Simply change the property this.price to this._price in the constructor. After that, create a getter to access this._price and a setter that will replace any non-numeric characters with nothing, leaving only the integers. This isn't perfect because it would strip out decimal points, but it's good for this demo.

classes/get/get.js
```
class Coupon {
  constructor(price, expiration) {
    this._price = price;
    this.expiration = expiration || 'Two Weeks';
  }
```

```
  get priceText() {
    return `$${this._price}`;
  }

  get price() {
    return this._price;
  }

  set price(price) {
    const newPrice = price
      .toString()
      .replace(/[^\d]/g, '');
    this._price = newPrice;
  }

  get expirationMessage() {
    return `This offer expires in ${this.expiration}`;
  }
}
const coupon = new Coupon(5);
coupon.price;
// 5

coupon.price = '$10';

coupon.price;
// 10

coupon.priceText;
// $ 10
export default Coupon;
```

A bonus to using this approach is you don't need to refactor any existing code. All code that currently uses coupon.price will work as intended.

The big advantage with getters and setters is that you hide complexity. The downside is that you mask your intentions. If another developer is writing code elsewhere, they may think they're setting a property when they're actually calling a method. Getters and setters can sometimes be very hard to debug and hard to test. As always, use with caution and make sure your intentions are clear with plenty of tests and documentation.

In the next tip, you'll learn another technique to mask complexity by turning data structures into iterables with generators.

Tip 41

Create Iterable Properties with Generators

In this tip, you'll learn how to convert complex data structures to iterables with generators.

In Tip 14, *Iterate Over Key-Value Data with Map and the Spread Operator*, on page 60, you learned how simple it is to loop over maps thanks to iterables. And once you can iterate over a collection, you have access to the spread operator, array methods, and many other tools to transform your data. Iterables give your data more flexibility by allowing you to access each piece of data individually.

You also know that objects don't have a built-in iterator. You can't loop over an object directly—you need to convert part of it to an array first. That can be a major problem when you want the structure of an object but the flexibility of an iterable.

In this tip, you'll learn a technique that can make complex data structures as easy to use as simple arrays. You're going to use a new specialized function called a generator to return data one piece at time. In the process, you'll see how you can convert a deeply nested object into a simple structure.

Generators aren't exclusive to classes. They're a specialized function. At the same time, they're very different from other functions. And while the JavaScript community has enthusiastically embraced most new features, they haven't quite figured out what to do with generators. In late 2016, a poll by Kent Dodds, a popular JavaScript developer, found that 81 percent of developers rarely or never used generators.[4]

That's changing. Developers and library authors are discovering how to use generators. One of the best use cases so far is to use generators to transform objects into iterables.

What is a generator? The Mozilla Developer Network explains that a generator is a function that doesn't fully execute its body immediately when called.[5]

---

4.   https://twitter.com/kentcdodds/status/775447130391535616

5.   https://developer.mozilla.org/en-US/docs/Web/JavaScript/Reference/Statements/function*

Finding Real Life Use Cases

Now that the JavaScript spec is updating yearly, you'll see new features regularly. Occasionally, you'll come across new syntax and have no idea why it was included or where you should use it. Sometimes it takes time to understand how to incorporate new syntax. When you find yourself stuck with new syntax that you don't understand, you should spend some time looking for real-life use cases.

The best way to find use cases for new syntax is to explore open source libraries. I usually have a few large projects—React, Redux, Lodash—that I search for syntax examples. All you need to do is go to GitHub, Gitlab, or anywhere the project is hosted and search for the syntax. When I was trying to learn how to use Map, I went to React and searched for new Map and found a few good examples. I discovered this generator pattern by looking through Khan Academy on github.

You'll quickly see a lot of usage patterns. And if you don't see many examples, that's a clue that the syntax may not be very valuable or at least not widely understood.

This is different from a higher-order function, which fully executes but returns a new function. A generator is a single function that doesn't resolve its body immediately. What that means is that a generator is a function that has break points where it essentially pauses until the next step.

To make a generator, you add an asterisk (*) after the function keyword. You then have access to a special method called next(), which returns a part of the function. Inside the function body, you return a piece of information with the keyword yield. When executing the function, use the next() method to get the information yielded by the function.

When you call next(), you get an object containing two keys: value and done. The item you declare with yield is the value. done indicates there are no items left.

For example, if you wanted to read Nobel Prize winner Naguib Mahfouz's Cairo Trilogy but you only wanted to know the titles one at a time, you'd write a function that would return the yields for each book in the trilogy. Each time you called yield(), you'd give the next book in the sequence.

To use the trilogy generator, you'd first have to call the function and assign it to a variable. You'd then call next() on the variable each time you wanted a new book.

classes/generators/simple.js
```js
function* getCairoTrilogy() {
  yield 'Palace Walk';
  yield 'Palace of Desire';
  yield 'Sugar Street';
}
```

```
const trilogy = getCairoTrilogy();
trilogy.next();
// { value: 'Palace Walk', done: false }
trilogy.next();
// { value: 'Palace of Desire', done: false }
trilogy.next();
// { value: 'Sugar Street', done: false }
trilogy.next();
// { value: undefined, done: true }
```

Notice how interesting that is. You can step through the function piece by piece. This is useful if you have lots of information and want to access it in parts. You could pull out one piece of information and pass the generator somewhere else to get the next piece. Like a higher-order function, you can use it in different places.

But that is not going to be your focus for this tip. Instead, it is far more interesting that generators turn a function into an iterable. Because you are accessing data one piece at a time, it is a simple step to turn them into iterables.

When you use a generator as an iterable, you don't need to use the next() method. Use any action that requires an iterable. The generator will go through the parts one at a time as if it were going through the indexes of an array or the keys of a map.

For example, if you want the Cairo trilogy in the form of an array, you'd simply use the spread operator.

classes/generators/simple.js
```
[...getCairoTrilogy];
// [ 'Palace Walk', 'Palace of Desire', 'Sugar Street']
```

If you want to add all the books to your reading list, all you'd need is a simple for...of loop.

classes/generators/simple.js
```
const readingList = {
  'Visit from the Goon Squad': true,
  'Manhattan Beach': false,
};
for (const book of getCairoTrilogy()) {
  readingList[book] = false;
}
readingList;
// {
//   'Visit from the Goon Squad': true,
//   'Manhattan Beach': false,
//   'Palace Walk': false,
```

```
//    'Palace of Desire': false,
//    'Sugar Street': false
// }
```

How does this fit into classes? Generators are awesome because, like getters and setters, they can give your classes a simple interface. You can make a class with a complex data structure but design it in such a way that developers using it will be able to access the data as if it were a simple array.

Consider a simple data structure: a family tree with a single branch. A person in a family tree would have a name and children. And each child would have children of their own.

A tree data structure would have advantages for searches and lookups, but flattening the information would be pretty difficult. You'd have to make a method to create an empty array and fill it with family members before returning.

```
classes/generators/problem.js
class FamilyTree {
  constructor() {
    this.family = {
      name: 'Dolores',
      child: {
        name: 'Martha',
        child: {
          name: 'Dyan',
          child: {
            name: 'Bea',
          },
        },
      },
    };
  }
  getMembers() {
    const family = [];
    let node = this.family;
    while (node) {
      family.push(node.name);
      node = node.child;
    }
    return family;
  }
}

const family = new FamilyTree();
family.getMembers();
// ['Dolores', 'Martha', 'Dyan', 'Bea'];

export default FamilyTree;
```

With a generator, you can return the data directly without pushing it to an array. As a bonus, your users wouldn't need to look up a method name. They could treat the property holding the family tree as if it were holding an array.

Converting the method to a generator is simple. You're just combining ideas from the method with ideas from your getCairoTrilogy() generator.

Start off by changing the method name from getMembers() to * [Symbol.iterator](). It looks confusing, but here's what's happening. First, the asterisk signifies that you're creating a generator. The phrase Symbol.iterator is attaching the generator to an iterable on the class. This is similar to how the map object has a MapIterator.

Inside the body of the method, add the while loop. Unlike your getCairoTrilogy() generator, you aren't going to yield an explicit value. Instead, you'll yield the value from each cycle of the loop. As long as there's something to return, the generator will keep going.

Instead of family.push(node.name);, all you need to do is yield the result: yield node.name. This means you don't need the intermediate array. Delete that. Everything else is the same

Now when you need any action that requires an iterable, such as the spread or the for...of loop, you can call it directly on the class instance.

```
classes/generators/generators.js
class FamilyTree {
  constructor() {
    this.family = {
      name: 'Dolores',
      child: {
        name: 'Martha',
        child: {
          name: 'Dyan',
          child: {
            name: 'Bea',
          },
        },
      },
    };
  }
  * [Symbol.iterator]() {
    let node = this.family;
    while (node) {
      yield node.name;
      node = node.child;
    }
  }
}
```

```
const family = new FamilyTree();
[...family];
// ['Dolores', 'Martha', 'Dyan', 'Bea'];
```

Is the extra complexity of the generator worth it? It depends on your goals. The advantage with a generator is that other developers don't need to get caught up in the implementation details of your class. They don't need to know that the class is actually using a tree data structure. To them, the class contains an iterable.

Of course, sometimes hiding complexity makes debugging more difficult. As with getters and setters, be careful about hiding too much from other developers. Still, when you want to use more complicated data structures but you don't want to burden others with implementation details, generators are a great solution.

In the next tip, you'll see how context problems can sneak into classes and how you can solve them using bind().

Tip 42

Resolve Context Problems with Bind()

In this tip, you'll learn how to solve this errors with bind().

In Tip 36, *Prevent Context Confusion with Arrow Functions*, on page 171, you saw how functions create a new context and how a new context can give you results you aren't expecting. Changing context can create confusion, particularly when you're using the this keyword in callbacks or array methods.

Sadly, the problem doesn't go away in classes. Earlier, you learned how you can use arrow functions to create another function without a new context. In this tip, you'll learn more techniques for preventing context problems. The techniques you're about to learn work on object literals and classes, but they're much more common in class syntax, particularly if you're using libraries such at React or Angular.

Think back to the original example, a validator. Originally, you made it as an object literal, but now that you know a bit about classes, you can make it a class. The class will have one property, a message, and two methods: setInvalidMessage(), which returns a single invalid message for a field, and setInvalidMessages(), which maps an array of fields to a series of invalid messages.

```
classes/bind/problem.js
class Validator {
  constructor() {
    this.message = 'is invalid.';
  }

  setInvalidMessage(field) {
    return `${field} ${this.message}`;
  }

  setInvalidMessages(...fields) {
    return fields.map(this.setInvalidMessage);
  }
}
```

All you did was translate an object with properties and methods to a class with properties and methods.

The Validator class will have the exact same context problem as your object. When you call setInvalidMessages(), the function creates a this binding to the class. Inside the method, you call map() on an array and pass setInvalidMessage() as the callback. When the map() method invokes setInvalidMessage(), it will create a new this binding in the context of the array method, not the class.

```
classes/bind/bind.spec.js
const validator = new ValidatorProblem();
validator.setInvalidMessages('city');
// TypeError: Cannot read property 'message' of undefined
```

Context problems are common in the React community. Nearly every class has some form of binding problem. Cory House has a great breakdown of different ways to solve the binding problem in React.[6] You'll be seeing an adaptation of most of those solutions in a more generic class.

The first way to solve the problem is the same as the solution suggested in Tip 36, *Prevent Context Confusion with Arrow Functions*, on page 171. Convert your method to an arrow function. The arrow function won't create a new this binding and it won't throw an error.

The only downside to this approach is that when you're working with class syntax, you'll have to move your function to a property rather than a method. It's not a big deal on objects because objects and properties both use a key-value declaration. In classes, you have to set properties in the constructor and the method will look a little out of place. Now you're stuck with a situation where some methods are set in the constructor and some are set as class methods.

```
classes/bind/constructorArrow.js
class Validator {
  constructor() {
    this.message = 'is invalid.';
    this.setInvalidMessage = field => `${field} ${this.message}`;
  }

  setInvalidMessages(...fields) {
    return fields.map(this.setInvalidMessage);
  }
}
```

Moving the method to a property in the constructor may solve your context problem, but it creates another. Methods are defined in multiple places. And depending on how many methods you create this way, your constructor can get large quickly.

A better solution is to use the bind() method. This method exists on all functions and lets you state your context explicitly. You'll always know what this refers to because you tell the function exactly where to bind.

---

6. https://medium.freecodecamp.org/react-binding-patterns-5-approaches-for-handling-this-92c651b5af56

As an example, suppose you have a function that refers to a property on this. The function doesn't actually have that property. The property this refers to may not yet exist. There's no rule that says properties must exist when you declare a function. But they do need to exist at runtime when you call a function or else you'll get undefined. With this function, you can explicitly set this to a specific object using bind.

```
classes/bind/bind.js
function sayMessage() {
  return this.message;
}

const alert = {
  message: 'Danger!',
};

const sayAlert = sayMessage.bind(alert);

sayAlert();
// Danger!
```

Whenever the function uses this, it will lock in the object you bound to it. Kyle Simpson calls this explicit binding because you're declaring the context and not relying on the engine to set it at runtime.[7]

In the preceding example, you're binding the sayMessage() function explicitly to an object that has the message property.

Now it's time for things to get a little confusing. You can also bind a function to the current context by binding it to this. It may seem odd to bind a this to, well, this, but all you're doing is telling the function to use the current context rather than creating a new one. Unlike an arrow function, the function is still creating a this binding—it's just using the current binding rather than building a new one.

In your Validator class, you can bind the function to the current context before you pass it to the map() method.

```
classes/bind/bind.js
class Validator {
  constructor() {
    this.message = 'is invalid.';
  }

  setInvalidMessage(field) {
    return `${field} ${this.message}`;
  }
```

---

7.   https://github.com/getify/You-Dont-Know-JS/blob/master/this%20%26%20object%20prototypes/
      ch2.md#explicit-binding

```
  setInvalidMessages(...fields) {
    return fields.map(this.setInvalidMessage.bind(this));
  }
}
```

That's a fine approach. The only downside is if you use the function in another method, you'll have to bind it again. A lot of developers avoid multiple binds by setting a bound method to a property of the same name in the constructor.

This is very similar to creating an arrow function in the constructor. The advantage is that your methods are still defined in the same place. They're merely bound in the constructor. Now you define all your methods in one place, the body. You declare your properties in another place, the constructor. And you set your context in one place, also the constructor.

classes/bind/constructor.js
```
class Validator {
  constructor() {
    this.message = 'is invalid.';
    this.setInvalidMessage = this.setInvalidMessage.bind(this);
  }

  setInvalidMessage(field) {
    return `${field} ${this.message}`;
  }

  setInvalidMessages(...fields) {
    return fields.map(this.setInvalidMessage);
  }
}
```

Both approaches—using arrow functions and binding a function to this— work with the current spec. In a future spec, you'll be able to set class properties outside of the constructor. With the new spec, you assign arrow functions to properties alongside other method definitions. It's the best of both worlds.

classes/bind/properties.js
```
class Validator {
  message = 'is invalid.';

  setMessage = field => `${field} ${this.message}`;

  setInvalidMessages(...fields) {
    return fields.map(this.setMessage);
  }
}
```

As with other proposed specs, you can use this feature right now with the proper Babel plugin. This particular feature isn't currently supported in any version of Node.js, so you won't be able to try it out in the REPL.

As with other context problems, try not to get too hung up on the details. Binding will make more sense when you see it organically. Just remember: If you're encountering unexpected behaviors or weird errors when using this, you might want to explicitly bind the context. Until that point, don't worry. Binding can be expensive, and you really should only use it when you need to solve a specific problem.

At this point, you should be able to create and extend classes with ease. Despite the controversy, it makes writing JavaScript a lot more intuitive for those outside the language and more succinct for those who've been developing JavaScript for years.

In the next chapter, you'll learn how to work with data outside your code by exploring promises, fetch methods, and asynchronous functions.

CHAPTER 9

Access External Data

In the 19th century, an international team of engineers embarked on one of the greatest engineering challenges of their day: laying a telegraph cable across the Atlantic Ocean. The project took several failed attempts and plenty of money and hours before it succeeded. In the end, you could send a message from Europe to the United States in an impressive 17 hours—much faster than the nearly two-week boat trip it used to take.

Fast communication can mean the difference between success and failure. JavaScript's resurgence is partially due to the fact that you can load a page once and then use JavaScript for all future communications to and from servers. Suddenly, you could experience websites as actual software instead of a series of discrete pages. When you skip page loads, you save time and resources for your users. They don't have to reload new images and other assets. They have less latency, and their experience is greatly improved. Accessing external data is crucial to so-called Single Page web applications.

In this chapter, you'll learn how to access external data and how to use the data you receive. JavaScript is an asynchronous language, which means it won't block code execution while waiting for requested data. JavaScript can give you speedy websites, but asynchronous requests can be a little confusing to work with.

We'll start off by exploring how to use fetch() to access remote data. Next, we'll take a deep dive into promises, the JavaScript method for handling asynchronous requests. Then we'll use the new async/await syntax to make working with promises even more clear. Finally, you'll learn to store data on the browser so you can keep a user's state without any server access.

You'll never experience performance gains on the level of the transatlantic cable, but every second counts. Don't be surprised when a mobile user leaves a site that requires a new page render on every action. You can't remove the server entirely, but you can give your users experiences that make the server requests as painless as possible.

Tip 43

Retrieve Data Asynchronously with Promises

In this tip, you'll learn how to work with delayed data responses using promises.

JavaScript is an asynchronous language. That's a big word for a simple concept. An asynchronous language is merely a language that can execute subsequent lines of code when previous lines of code aren't fully resolved.

All right. Maybe that explanation wasn't any more clear. Think about reasons why code may be blocked. You may be getting data from an API. You might be pulling data from the DOM or other source. You might be waiting for a user response. The common thread is you need some information to proceed, and it may take time to get it. If you want more examples, Peter Olson has a great breakdown of the differences between asynchronous and synchronous code.[1]

The value of asynchronous languages is that if there are parts of your code that don't require the delayed information, you can run the code while the other code is waiting. If you're waiting for an API response, you can still respond to click methods on other elements or calculate values of other data sources. Your code doesn't grind to a halt while waiting.

In later tips, you'll work with API data specifically. In this tip, you'll explore a reusable technique for working with asynchronous data: promises.

Before promises, developers used callbacks to handle asynchronous actions. If you requested expenses from a data source, you'd pass a callback function as an argument. After the asynchronous data is returned—or resolved as it is often called—the function would execute the callback. The traditional example is a setTimeout() function that takes a callback and executes it after a certain number of milliseconds.

Use setTimeout() as a place holder for any action that doesn't immediately resolve. For example, think about a function called getUserPreferences(), which would fetch data from an API and then pass that data to a callback.

Because Javascript is asynchronous, you can call other functions before and after the call to getUserPreferences() and they'd both resolve before getUserPreferences() executes the callback.

---

1. https://www.pluralsight.com/guides/front-end-javascript/introduction-to-asynchronous-javascript

externalData/promises/problem.js
```javascript
function getUserPreferences(cb) {
  setTimeout(() => {
    cb({
      theme: 'dusk',
    });
  }, 1000);
}

function log(value) {
  return console.log(value);
}

log('starting');
// starting

getUserPreferences(preferences => {
  return log(preferences.theme.toUpperCase());
});

log('ending?');
// ending

// DUSK
```

Callbacks are a fine way to handle asynchronous data. And they were a standard tool for a long time. The problem is that you may have asynchronous functions that call asynchronous functions, that call asynchronous… Eventually you have so many nested callbacks, you find yourself in what became known as "callback hell."

What if you wanted to get a music selection based on a user's preference? The callback function, getMusic(), also needs to hit an API and also needs a callback based on the API response. You encounter this situation all the time. Here's your getMusic() function:

externalData/promises/problem.js
```javascript
function getMusic(theme, cb) {
  setTimeout(() => {
    if (theme === 'dusk') {
      return cb({
        album: 'music for airports',
      });
    }
    return cb({
      album: 'kind of blue',
    });
  }, 1000);
}
```

Now you need to get the preference and then get an album. First, you'd make a call to getUserPreferences() and you'd pass getMusic() as a callback. getMusic() takes a theme preference and a callback. This function is only nested two deep, and it's already getting hard to read.

externalData/promises/problem.js
```
getUserPreferences(preferences => {
  return getMusic(preferences.theme, music => {
    console.log(music.album);
  });
});
```

As if that weren't enough, many asynchronous functions took two callbacks: a callback for a successful response and a callback for an error. Things got complicated fast.

Promises solve the callback problem twice over. Instead of taking callback functions as arguments, promises have methods for success and failure. This keeps things visually flat. In addition, you can chain together asynchronous promises instead of nesting them. This means that you can neatly stack all of your actions.

How does it work? A promise is an object that takes asynchronous action and calls one of two methods based on the response. If the asynchronous action is successful, or fulfilled, the promise passes the results to a then() method. If the action fails, or is rejected, the promise calls the catch() method. Both then() and catch() take a function as an argument, and that can only take a single response argument.

A promise takes two arguments: resolve() and reject(). resolve() is what happens when things go as planned. When resolve() is called, the code will execute the function passed to the then() method. When you define your getUserPreferences() function, you'll return the promise. When you actually call getUserPreferences(), you'll call either the then() or the catch() method.

externalData/promises/promises.js
```
function getUserPreferences() {
  const preferences = new Promise((resolve, reject) => {
    resolve({
      theme: 'dusk',
    });
  });
  return preferences;
}
```

Here's an example of calling a code and running a function on successful resolution using the then() method.

externalData/promises/promises.js
```
getUserPreferences()
  .then(preferences => {
    console.log(preferences.theme);
  });
// 'dusk'
```

In this case, things went well, but you should always have a backup plan. Whenever you set up a promise, you can have both a then() and a catch() method. The then() method will handle the resolutions. The catch() method will handle the rejections.

Here's a failing promise. Note that it's calling the reject() argument.

externalData/promises/promises.js
```
function failUserPreference() {
  const finder = new Promise((resolve, reject) => {
    reject({
      type: 'Access Denied',
    });
  });
  return finder;
}
```

When you call a promise, you can add attach the then() method and the catch() using chaining.

externalData/promises/promises.js
```
failUserPreference()
  .then(preferences => {
  // This won't execute
    console.log(preferences.theme);
  })
  .catch(error => {
    console.error(`Fail: ${error.type}`);
  });
// Fail: Access Denied
```

This code should already look more clean. The fun really begins when you chain multiple promises together.

Remember your getMusic() function? Try converting that to a promise.

externalData/promises/promises.js
```
function getMusic(theme) {
  if (theme === 'dusk') {
    return Promise.resolve({
      album: 'music for airports',
```

```
    });
  }
  return Promise.resolve({
    album: 'kind of blue',
  });
}
```

After you do, you can call and return it in the then() method of getUserPreferences().
After you do that, you can call another then() method, which will call a function
using the results from getMusic().

```
getUserPreferences()
  .then(preference => {
    return getMusic(preference.theme);
  })
  .then(music => {
    console.log(music.album);
  });
// music for airports
```

See what's happening? Instead of passing data into a series of nested callbacks, you're passing data down through a series of then() methods.

And, of course, because you're returning promises, you can convert everything
to single-line arrow functions with an implicit return.

```
getUserPreferences()
  .then(preference => getMusic(preference.theme))
  .then(music => { console.log(music.album); });
```

Finally, as if that weren't enough, if you're chaining promises together, you
don't need to add a catch() method to each one. You can define a single catch()
method to handle a case where *any* promise is rejected.

To see a chained catch() in action, create another promise that returns the
artist for an album.

```
function getArtist(album) {
  return Promise.resolve({
    artist: 'Brian Eno',
  });
}
```

Unfortunately, you won't get to use getArtists() because getMusic() is going to be
rejected. Don't worry—it won't kill your code. Your code will execute the catch()
at the bottom of the group even though it was defined after another then()
method.

externalData/promises/promises.js
```javascript
function failMusic(theme) {
  return Promise.reject({
    type: 'Network error',
  });
}

getUserPreferences()
  .then(preference => failMusic(preference.theme))
  .then(music => getArtist(music.album))
  .catch(e => {
    console.log(e);
  });
```

As you can see, promises can handle a lot of situations with a very simple interface. There's even a method called Promise.all that takes an array of promises and returns either a resolve or a reject when they all finish.[2]

Promises took the JavaScript world by storm. They're an amazing tool that can help you make otherwise ugly code gorgeous and easy to read.

Of course, things can always get better. In ES2017, the TC39 committee approved a new method for handling asynchronous functions. Well, it's actually a two-step process called async/await and it takes asynchronous data in an interesting new direction.

In the next tip, you'll explore async/await and see how you can make your asynchronous code even more readable.

---

2.   https://developer.mozilla.org/en-US/docs/Web/JavaScript/Reference/Global_Objects/Promise/all

Create Clean Functions with Async/Await

In this tip, you'll learn how to streamline promises with async/await.

In the previous tip, you saw that promises are awesome. They're a vast improvement over callbacks, but their interfaces are still a little clunky. You're still working with callbacks in methods. Fortunately, the language continues to improve. You can now avoid callbacks entirely by adding asynchronous promise data to a variable in a single function.

Developers usually talk about the new syntax, async/await, as a group, but it's really two separate actions. You use the async keyword to declare that an encapsulating function will be using asynchronous data. Inside the asynchronous function, you can use the await keyword to pause the function until a value is returned.

Before you begin, there are a couple things to note. First, this doesn't replace promises. You're merely wrapping promises in a better syntax. Second, it isn't well supported, and the compiled code is a little buggy. It's safe to use on server-side JavaScript, but you may have problems in browsers.

To see async/await in action, refactor some of your code from the previous tip. As a reminder, you pass a function to the then() method on the getUserPreferences() function.

```
externalData/promises/promises.js
getUserPreferences()
  .then(preferences => {
    console.log(preferences.theme);
  });
// 'dusk'
```

First, you'll need to wrap the call to getUserPreferences() in another function. Write a new function called getTheme(). This will hold all of your calls to asynchronous functions. To indicate that you'll be calling asynchronous functions, add the async keyword right before the function keyword.

Inside your getTheme() function, you can call getUserPreferences(). Before you call the function, though, add the await keyword to signal that getUserPreferences() will return a promise. This allows you to assign the resolved promise to a new variable.

externalData/async/async.js
```
async function getTheme() {
  const { theme } = await getUserPreferences();
  return theme;
}
```

The trick with an asynchronous function is that it's transformed into a promise. In other words, when you call getTheme(), you'll still need a then() method.

externalData/async/async.js
```
getTheme()
  .then(theme => {
    console.log(theme);
  });
```

You cleaned things up a little, but honestly, not much. async functions really shine when you're working with multiple promises.

Think about the previous tip when you chained multiple promises together. With async/await, you can assign each return statement to a variable before passing the variable to the next function. In other words, you can transform your chained promises into a series of function calls in a single wrapping function. Try creating a new function called getArtistsByPreference() where you call a series of asynchronous functions passing the data from the previous function as an argument to the next.

externalData/async/async.js
```
async function getArtistByPreference() {
  const { theme } = await getUserPreferences();
  const { album } = await getMusic(theme);
  const { artist } = await getArtist(album);
  return artist;
}

getArtistByPreference()
  .then(artist => {
    console.log(artist);
  });
```

That's a vast improvement over a long method chain.

All that's left is handling errors. In this case, you'll need to move error handling outside the wrapping function. Instead, you still use the catch method when you're invoking getArtistsByPreference(). Because getArtistsByPreference() returns a promise, you need to add a catch() method in case *any* of your internal asynchronous functions return an error.

externalData/async/catch.js

```
async function getArtistByPreference() {
  const { theme } = await getUserPreferences();
  const { album } = await failMusic(theme);
  const { artist } = await getArtist(album);
  return artist;
}

getArtistByPreference()
  .then(artist => {
    console.log(artist);
  })
  .catch(e => {
    console.error(e);
  });
```

async/await functions can clean up your code, but again, use them with caution, particularly when you're compiling your code to earlier versions of JavaScript.

At this point, you have a few tools for handling asynchronous actions, but you're probably wondering when you'll actually use them. You use promises in many situations, but the most common is when you're fetching data from an API.

In the next tip, you'll learn how to access data from an endpoint using fetch.

Tip 45

Make Simple AJAX Calls with Fetch

In this tip, you'll learn how to retrieve remote data using fetch().

If you do any significant JavaScript app development, you'll have to interact with APIs. With APIs, you can get current information and update single elements without a page refresh. In short, you can create very fast applications that behave like native software.

Single-page web apps are part of the reason why JavaScript is so popular, but getting data with AJAX—Asynchronous JavaScript And XML—used to be a hassle. It was such a hassle that most developers used a library, usually jQuery, to to reduce the complexity. You can see the documentation on the Mozilla Developer Network.[3] It's not easy stuff.

Now, there's a much simpler tool for AJAX calls: fetch(). This tip is a little different than the others. fetch() isn't part of the JavaScript spec. The fetch spec is defined by the Web Hypertext Application Technology Working Group or WHATWG.[4] That means you'll be able to find it in most major browsers, but it isn't natively supported in Node.js. If you want to use it in Node.js, you'll need to use the node-fetch package.[5]

Enough trivia. How does it work?

To start, you need an endpoint. The good folks at typicode have an API for fake blog data at https://jsonplaceholder.typicode.com/. They also make an amazing tool called JSON Server that enables you to mock APIs locally.[6] JSON Server is a great way to mock APIs that are in development or slow, require authentication, or cost money for each call. You should use it.

Now that you have an endpoint, it's time to make some requests.

The first request you'll make is a simple GET request. If all you're doing is asking for data, the fetch() call is simple. Call fetch() with the endpoint URL as the argument:

---

3.   https://developer.mozilla.org/en-US/docs/AJAX/Getting_Started
4.   https://fetch.spec.whatwg.org/
5.   https://www.npmjs.com/package/node-fetch
6.   https://github.com/typicode/json-server

externalData/fetch/fetch.js
```js
fetch('https://jsonplaceholder.typicode.com/posts/1');
```

The response body for this endpoint will be information about a blog post:

externalData/fetch/fetch.js
```js
{
  userId: 1,
  id: 1,
  title: 'First Post',
  body: 'This is my first post...',
};
```

You can't get much easier than that. After you make the request, fetch() will return a promise that resolves with a response. The next thing you'll need to do is add a callback function to the then() method to handle the response.

Ultimately, you want to get the response body. But the response object contains quite a bit of information beyond the body, including the status code, headers, and more. You'll see more about the response in a moment.

The response body isn't always in a usable format. You may need to convert it to a format JavaScript can handle. Fortunately, fetch() contains a number of mixins that will automatically convert the response body data. In this case, because you know you're getting JSON, you can convert the body to JSON by calling json() on the response. The method also returns a promise, so you'll need another then() method. After that, you can do something with the parsed data. For example, if you want the title only, you can pull it out.

externalData/fetch/fetch.js
```js
fetch('https://jsonplaceholder.typicode.com/posts/1')
  .then(data => {
    return data.json();
  })
  .then(post => {
    console.log(post.title);
  });
```

Of course, nothing is ever easy. The fetch() promise will resolve even if you get a failing status code, such as a 404 response. In other words, you can't rely on a catch() method on the promise to handle failed requests.

The response does include a field called ok that's set to true if the response code is in the 200–299 range. You can check for that response and throw an error if there's a problem. Unfortunately, Internet Explorer doesn't include ok, but Edge does. If you need to support older versions of Internet Explorer, you can check response.status to see if the value is between 200 and 299.

externalData/fetch/fetch.js

```
fetch('https://jsonplaceholder.typicode.com/pots/1')
  .then(data => {
    if (!data.ok) {
      throw Error(data.status);
    }
    return data.json();
  })
  .then(post => {
    console.log(post.title);
  })
  .catch(e => {
    console.log(e);
  });
```

Most of your requests will be simple GET requests. But you'll eventually need to make more complex requests. What if you wanted to add a new blog post? Easy, make a POST request to https://jsonplaceholder.typicode.com/posts.

Once you move beyond GET requests, you'll need to set a few more options. So far, you've only supplied a single argument to fetch()—the URL endpoint. Now you'll need to pass an object of configuration options as a second argument. The optional object can take a lot of different details. In this case, include only the most necessary information.

Because you're sending a POST request, you'll need to declare that you're using the POST method. In addition, you'll need to pass some JSON data to actually create the new blog post. Because you're sending JSON data, you'll need to set a header of Content-Type set to application/json. Finally, you'll need the body, which will be a single string of JSON data.

The final request is nearly identical to your other request, except you pass in the special options as the second argument.

externalData/fetch/fetch.js

```
const update = {
  title: 'Clarence White Techniques',
  body: 'Amazing',
  userId: 1,
};

const options = {
  method: 'POST',
  headers: {
    'Content-Type': 'application/json',
  },
  body: JSON.stringify(update),
};
```

```
fetch('https://jsonplaceholder.typicode.com/posts', options).then(data => {
  if (!data.ok) {
    throw Error(data.status);
  }
  return data.json();
}).then(update => {
  console.log(update);
  // {
  //   title: 'Clarence White Techniques',
  //   body: 'Amazing',
  //   userId: 1,
  //   id: 101
  // };
}).catch(e => {
  console.log(e);
});
```

If your request is successful, you'll get a response body containing the blog post object along with a new ID. The response will vary depending on how the API is set up.

While JSON data is probably the most common request body, there are other options, such as FormData. Beyond that, there are even more methods for customizing your request. You can set a mode, a cache method, and so on. Most of these are specialized, but you'll need them at some point. As always, the best place to find out more is the Mozilla Developer Network.[7]

Finally, you should be careful about where you place your AJAX requests in your code. Remember that fetch will most likely need an Internet connection, and endpoints may change during the project. It's good practice to keep all your fetch actions in one location. This will make them easier to update and easier to test. Check out the code for the book to see how you can create a services directory to store your fetch functions and how you can use them in other functions.

In the next tip, you'll learn how to preserve user data with localStorage.

---

7.   https://developer.mozilla.org/en-US/docs/Web/API/Fetch_API/Using_Fetch

Tip 46

Maintain State Over Time with LocalStorage

In this tip, you'll learn how to save user data with localStorage.

Users love to personalize applications. Conversely, they hate entering the same data every time they visit an app or a page. When you're working with front-end JavaScript, you're in a bit of a bind. How do you preserve user data with minimal interference?

An obvious solution is to create a login. The problem is that many users will abandon a site if they're forced to log in. A better, albeit imperfect, solution is to store data locally. When you save data locally, you can preserve information on a particular browser on a particular device.

Of course, everyone uses multiple devices. So saving data to a browser won't help a user who works across multiple devices. Still, it's far less intrusive than demanding a user make yet another account.

You can easily save user information with localStorage. localStorage is like a tiny database that exists only in your browser. You can add and retrieve information from it, but it isn't accessible by JavaScript in the browser.

Think back to your pet adoption site from Tip 13, *Update Key-Value Data Clearly with Maps*, on page 54. You set up a series of filters to show only relevant pets. Because pet owners tend to prefer certain types of animals—lovers of labradors probably won't look for tiny dogs—you could do them a favor if you save their searches between sessions.

Start by saving a breed preference. To save a breed, you just need to set the value on the localStorage object using the setItem() method. You pass the key as the first argument and the value as the second. The syntax should look familiar. It's nearly identical to the method for setting data on a map.

externalData/local/local.js
```
function saveBreed(breed) {
  localStorage.setItem('breed', breed);
}
```

When the user leaves and then returns to the page later, you can pull out the data with a similar command.

externalData/local/local.js
```
function getSavedBreed() {
  return localStorage.getItem('breed');
}
```

And if you want to remove an item, you can do that, too.

externalData/local/local.js
```
function removeBreed() {
  return localStorage.removeItem('breed');
}
```

Now think about why this is so powerful. You can save user data without requiring any extra effort from the user. That means that when they return to the page or even refresh the page, you can set the application exactly as they left it.

For example, when you initialize your filters, you can add in the breed information from localStorage if it exists.

externalData/local/local.js
```
function applyBreedPreference(filters) {
  const breed = getSavedBreed();
  if (breed) {
    filters.set('breed', breed);
  }
  return filters;
}
```

Like any object, you can have as many keys as you want. If you wanted to save all your user's filters, you could save each item individually, but it's much easier to save the whole group. It's already structured data, so why spend time taking it apart?

The only downside to localStorage is that your value must be a string. You can't save an array or an object in localStorage. Fortunately, the fix is simple. Just use JSON.stringify() to convert your data to a string and JSON.parse to convert it back to a JavaScript object.

If you wanted to save all of your user's search, you can convert all the filters to a string. Remember that because you were using a map, you'll need to spread it into an array first.

externalData/local/local.js
```
function savePreferences(filters) {
  const filterString = JSON.stringify([...filters]);
  localStorage.setItem('preferences', filterString);
}
```

When you want to use it, you'll just need to pull the data from localStorage and convert it back into a map. Of course, if you're saving objects or arrays, all you need to do is parse the string.

externalData/local/local.js
```
function retrievePreferences() {
  const preferences = JSON.parse(localStorage.getItem('preferences'));
  return new Map(preferences);
}
```

And, on occasion, you may just want to get back to a clean slate. In that case, you can remove all key-values with clear().

externalData/local/local.js
```
function clearPreferences() {
  localStorage.clear();
}
```

localStorage is one of those tools that's simple but incredibly powerful. It will make you users happy and it's simple to use. The data won't persist across devices, but the benefit of avoiding a login far outweighs this downside.

In addition, you can also temporarily save data with sessionStorage.[8] The usage is identical except sessionStorage doesn't persist after a tab is closed. This is a great tool when you have a project that mixes server-side rendering and client-side functionality. You can save preferences between page refreshes while also ensuring that the user will have fresh state when they return.

You now have the tools to make fully integrated single page applications. Between locally saved information and API access, you only need servers to render the page once. fetch() and localStorage are incredibly simple, but they open the door to limitless opportunities to create powerful software in the browser.

In the next chapter, you'll take a step back and look at how to architect and organize your code when building applications longer than a few lines of code.

---

8.   https://developer.mozilla.org/en-US/docs/Web/API/Window/sessionStorage

CHAPTER 10

Gather Related Files with Component Architecture

In chess, there's a distinction between tactics and strategy. Tactics are a series or combination of moves to achieve a goal. It's short term and fairly easy to define and teach. Strategy, by contrast, is an abstract conception of which side has more influence in a particular part of the board. Tactics solve problems at hand. Strategy allocates resources in anticipation of future problems.

Most coding books, including this one, are about tactics. How do you transform an array? How do you write a function that consumes asynchronous data?

Now you're going to learn strategy. In the software development world, organizing code in a way that makes it extendable, reusable, and manageable is called architecture. Instead of solving clear problems, you're going to learn to split and organize code to make future problems—extending classes, handling edge cases, finding bugs—easier to solve. You got a taste of code architecture when you learned about dependency injection in Tip 32, *Write Functions for Testability*, on page 151. That was the first time you saw how code could be split to keep one function focused and flexible.

Most books avoid discussing architecture because it's messy. The solutions aren't clear, and you can usually only recognize a mistake months later when it's too late and too expensive to change the structure of a codebase. In this chapter, you'll see how to structure a project from the ground up. You'll learn how to incorporate modern JavaScript tooling to pull the pieces together into a final product.

You'll start off by learning how you can separate code into different files using import and export. Next, you'll learn how to incorporate third-party code with npm. Then, you'll learn how to break an application into well-designed pieces using the component architecture pattern. This isn't the only architecture pattern, but it's the most popular one now, and it's very different from most server-side patterns.

Next, you'll combine the pieces into a final, usable asset with build tools. And you'll finish up by learning how to use CSS to handle animations that used to be the responsibility of JavaScript.

This chapter will be a little more difficult. There are more moving pieces, and the examples are more complex, even as they're still extremely simplified compared to anything you'll see in production. But if you come away understanding that clean architecture is just as important—and just as achievable—as clean code, I guarantee your projects will benefit.

The first step in creating a clean architecture is breaking code into reusable and shareable pieces with import and export.

Tip 47

Isolate Functionality with Import and Export

In this tip, you'll learn how to share code between files.

In the bad old days of JavaScript, you kept all code in a single file. Even worse, developers would put all their JavaScript code in the DOM under a single <script> tag.

Things got better slowly. First, someone created code to minify and concatenate files so at least you had only one small import statement. Then projects such as Require.js and CommonJS gave developers a way to share code between files using modules. With the module system, JavaScript developers were finally able to easily reuse code in a project.

Modules have been simplified and are now simple import and export statements. And with this simple interface, not only can you share code between files in a project, but you can also use community code with nearly identical syntax. You'll see more about community code in the next tip. For now, let's look at how to import and export code.

This code won't work out-of-the box. It's still a good idea to combine and minify your code to a single file. Eventually, browsers will be able to dynamically import code, but for now, you still need to create single files, often called bundles or packages. You'll see how in Tip 50, *Use Build Tools to Combine Components*, on page 240.

You've actually been using exported code throughout the book. You wouldn't know unless you looked at the book's source code because the examples hid the code export. Importing and exporting is just that simple. You export any existing code with a single statement.

Here's some code from Tip 36, *Prevent Context Confusion with Arrow Functions*, on page 171:

```
functions/context/method.js
const validator = {
  message: 'is invalid.',
  setInvalidMessage: field => `${field} ${this.message}`,
};
```

If you want to share the code, you just need to add a simple export statement.

functions/context/method.js

```
const validator = {
  message: 'is invalid.',
  setInvalidMessage: field => `${field} ${this.message}`,
};

export { validator };
```

How does it work? At the most basic level, all you need to do is export an object containing the data you want to share. That means you can export functions, variables, and classes. And you don't need to export anything. If you choose to export some functions and not others, you've essentially created public and private functions.

In the preceding example, you exported a single function. In other situations, you may have a function you don't want to share essentially making it private. In that situation, export all the functions you're willing to share.

Here's how it would look if you wanted to share two functions while hiding one:

architecture/import/single/util.js

```
function getPower(decimalPlaces) {
  return 10 ** decimalPlaces;
}

function capitalize(word) {
  return word[0].toUpperCase() + word.slice(1);
}

function roundToDecimalPlace(number, decimalPlaces = 2) {
  const round = getPower(decimalPlaces);
  return Math.round(number * round) / round;
}

export { capitalize, roundToDecimalPlace };
```

Now that you've exported the functions, you'll probably want to use them. To use a function in another file, use the import keyword and the functions you'd like to import to curly braces. After you declare what you're importing, give the path relative to the file you're in.

You can also import library code and you'll see how in the next tip. For now, you're only importing code from other files you own. Try importing some utility functions into a new file. It would look like this:

architecture/import/single/bill.js

```
import { capitalize, roundToDecimalPlace } from './util';

function giveTotal(name, total) {
  return `${capitalize(name)}, your total is: ${roundToDecimalPlace(total)}`;
}
```

```
giveTotal('sara', 10.3333333);
// "Sara, your total is: 10.33"

export { giveTotal };
```

You don't have to import everything. If you want only a single item, that's fine.

architecture/import/single/name.js
```
import { capitalize } from './util';

function greet(name) {
  return `Hello, ${capitalize(name)}!`;
}

greet('ashley');
// Hello, Ashley!

export { greet };
```

And you don't have to limit yourself to functions. You can also export variables and classes.

architecture/import/single/math.js
```
const PI = 3.14;
const E = 2.71828;

export { E, PI };
```

This probably looks familiar. Exporting and importing use nearly the same syntax as destructuring. In fact, if you want you keep all your imports as properties on an object, you simply import everything to a variable name.

The syntax is a little different from destructuring. Declare that you're importing all functions using the asterisks and then give the variable name. You can now call the functions as if they were on an object.

architecture/import/each/name.js
```
import * as utils from './util';

function greet(name) {
  return `Hello, ${utils.capitalize(name)}!`;
}

greet('ashley');
// Hello, Ashley!

export { greet };
```

As with destructuring, you can also rename functions or data you import. The syntax is slightly different. Instead of a colon, like you'd use in destructuring, you use the keyword as to assign the data to a new variable.

Exports are already simple, but there are a few shortcuts that make things even easier.

Instead of declaring an object and adding each piece of data at the end, you can add the export keyword before each function. This makes your code even easier because you don't need an object at the bottom of the file.

architecture/import/each/util.js
```
function getPower(decimalPlaces) {
  return 10 ** decimalPlaces;
}
export function capitalize(word) {
  return word[0].toUpperCase() + word.slice(1);
}
export function roundToDecimalPlace(number, decimalPlaces = 2) {
  const round = getPower(decimalPlaces);
  return Math.round(number * round) / round;
}
```

Exporting functions one at a time doesn't change how you import. You can use any of the techniques mentioned.

As you start to separate out your code, you'll often have files that contain a single entry point. Or you may have a function that's more important. In those situations, you can declare a default export. This will make the import process a little shorter.

Consider a file that converts an address object to a string. The main goal of the utility is to convert an object. There's a clear default export. But you may still want to share some helper functions.

Add the keyword default after the export keyword on normalize() to make it the main export. Add export to any remaining functions.

architecture/import/default/address.js
```
import { capitalize } from '../single/util';

export function parseRegion(address) {
  const region = address.state || address.providence || '';
  return region.toUpperCase();
}
export function parseStreet({ street }) {
  return street.split(' ')
    .map(part => capitalize(part))
    .join(' ');
}
export default function normalize(address) {
  const street = parseStreet(address);
  const city = address.city;
  const region = parseRegion(address);
  return `${street} ${city}, ${region}`;
}
```

Now when you want to import normalize(), you use the same syntax but without the curly braces. If you don't use curly braces, you'll get the default export and nothing else. You don't need to use the exact function name—you can import the default to any variable name you want—but it's a good idea to use the same name as the default to keep things readable.

architecture/import/default/mail.js

```
import normalize from './address';

function getAddress(user) {
  return normalize(user.address);
}

export default getAddress;
```

If you want to import the default function along with some other functions, you can mix and match import statements. Separate the default and the curly brace import using a comma.

architecture/import/default/list.js

```
import normalize, { parseRegion } from './address';

function getAddress(user) {
  return normalize(user.address);
}
export function getAddressByRegion(users) {
  return users.reduce((regions, user) => {
    const { address } = user;
    const region = parseRegion(address);
    const addresses = regions[region] || [];
    regions[region] = [...addresses, normalize(address)];
    return regions;
  }, {});
}
const bars = [
  {
    name: 'Saint Vitus',
    address: {
      street: '1120 manhattan ave',
      city: 'Brooklyn',
      state: 'NY',
    },
  },
];
getAddressByRegion(bars);
// {
//   NY: ["1120 Manhattan Ave Brooklyn, NY"]
// }
```

Default imports are particularly useful on classes because there should be only one class per file, so there's no reason to export other code.

architecture/import/class/address.js
```
import { capitalize } from '../single/util';

export default class Address {
  constructor(address) {
    this.address = address;
  }

  normalize() {
    const street = this.parseStreet(this.address);
    const city = this.address.city;
    const region = this.parseRegion(this.address);
    return `${street} ${city}, ${region}`;
  }

  parseStreet({ street }) {
    return street.split(' ')
      .map(part => capitalize(part))
      .join(' ');
  }

  parseRegion(address) {
    const region = address.state || address.providence || '';
    return region.toUpperCase();
  }
}
```

As you can see, imports and exports are so intuitive there's not really much to say. But there is one slight problem—because you can split code easily, your projects will start to grow. Don't worry, though. As your project grows, you can split code into different files. This will let you organize code more efficiently and logically. In Tip 49, *Build Applications with Component Architecture*, on page 235, you'll learn one way to organize code. But before you get to that point, you'll almost certainly want to use code outside your own codebase. Fortunately, that's easier than ever.

In the next tip, you'll learn how to use community code with npm.

Tip 48

Leverage Community Knowledge with npm

In this tip, you'll learn how to import external code with npm.

In the previous tip, you learned how to use code from different files. In this tip, you'll learn how to use community code created by developers all over the world.

Not many years ago, if you wanted to use an open source library, you were forced to either copy-paste code locally, download a library to your project, or include an external dependency using a <script> tag in your markup.

You'd get your code—unless an external source went down—but it was hard to keep dependencies up to date, particularly if you were storing them locally. Not only was it hard to maintain, but you also had to write your custom code assuming the library would be there. This made code really hard to read and test because you never explicitly included anything.

Those days are gone. You can now download code directly to your project, control versions, and import code into individual files using familiar conventions.

You manage all this with a tool called the node package manager, or npm. There are a few alternatives, such as Facebook's yarn project, but they work in mostly the same way, so don't worry too much about the differences.

npm is an important project, and you'll mostly use it for importing code, but it can do a lot more. With npm, you can set your project's metadata and configuration information, run command-line scripts, and even publish your project for others to use.

Before you begin, you'll need to have Node.js installed. But after that, you're ready to go. When you install Node.js, you also install npm.

After Node.js and npm are installed, you need to initialize a project. Open up a terminal, go to the root of your project, and type npm init. This will start up a configuration tool that will create a package.json file for you.

This package.json file will contain metadata information for your project, such as name, description, license, and so on. It will eventually contain all the external code dependencies. It's important to note that npm init only creates the package.json file. It doesn't set any other hidden files or directories. You don't need to worry about cluttering your file system.

If you aren't sure what you want, don't worry. You can change all of that information later. Go with the defaults at first if you have any doubts. When you finish, you'll have a file that looks like this:

architecture/npm/defaults/package.json
```
{
  "name": "test",
  "version": "1.0.0",
  "description": "",
  "main": "index.js",
  "scripts": {
    "test": "echo \"Error: no test specified\" && exit 1"
  },
  "author": "",
  "license": "ISC"
}
```

Pretty simple. It's just an object containing most of the information you just entered. The only surprise is the scripts field. This is where you'd add command-line scripts. You'll see some more of this in a bit.

Don't let the slimness of the file fool you. This is the most important entry point for a large JavaScript application. It's also where you store information about external dependencies.

Let's say you're building a collection with maps and you wanted to convert an object to a map. You could write some code to convert the object to a map, but you really just want a quick solution. With some research, you'd likely come across Lodash—a suite of tools for converting data.[1] How do you get the code into your project?

In addition to structuring your project, npm is also a resource for sharing code. Better still, npm tracks data such as number of downloads, number of open bugs, versions, and so on.

If you open the npm page for the Lodash package,[2] you'll see that it's been downloaded about 50 million times per month. In essence, 50 million projects are giving Lodash a stamp of approval.

The data collected by npm is a tacit endorsement by the greater JavaScript community. You don't need to avoid code from rarely used projects, but you may want to investigate the code before bringing it into your codebase. Fortunately, there's always a link to the code base, so you can check it out yourself if you aren't sure.

---

1. https://lodash.com/
2. https://www.npmjs.com/package/lodash

Evaluating Open Source Code

There's a lot of open source code in the world. But not all code is equal. npm doesn't approve code before it's published (although npm will remove malicious code) so you're responsible for evaluating code you want to include in your project.

The best place to start is the download count. If there's a large number of monthly downloads, it's probably safe code. Trust the community to do some of the vetting for you.

Next, look at the issue count. If there are lots of issues, that's a sign the project is poorly maintained. Keep bugs in context, though. A large project with lots of downloads will probably have more bugs due to sheer volume.

After that, dive into the open source code directly. npm will always have a link to the codebase. The code is usually on github, but you'll also see gitlab and bitbucket. Head over there and look through the project. The two most important things you'll see are the latest commit date and the pull requests.

If the code doesn't have a commit in the last six months, you should probably move on. It may be abandoned.

A pull request is when someone submits a code update. These must be approved by the maintainer before it's included. If there are stale merge requests, it's another clue that the code isn't well managed. Nothing is more frustrating than submitting a merge request and watching it linger for months or even years.

Finally, when in doubt, look at the actual code. Sometimes it's hard to find your way around, but it's a good exercise, and you can usually tell at a glance if the code is well-structured. If things are neat and organized, and follow standard conventions, then you're probably safe. If the code is cluttered with syntax errors, you should run away screaming. If you wouldn't accept the code in your own code base, don't include the project. After all, when you import the code, you *are* accepting it into your code base.

Trust your intuition. It's better to look for other projects or pull out parts of an open source library with good old copy-paste than to include a project that may be bloated or buggy.

Once you're satisfied that code is worth using, you can install it in your project by running npm install --save lodash. It's not strictly necessary to use the --save flag, but it's a good habit because there are two types of code you'll install. More on that in a bit.

The npm install command does a few things. If there isn't a node_modules directory, the command will create one and copy down the package. Next, it updates your package.json to include the version number of the code you're importing. Finally, it will create a package-lock.json file that includes detailed information about the version of the installed code along with any other libraries that the code requires.

When you install one package, you may actually install several packages. They'll all be in your package-lock.json or your node_modules/ directory. The original code you installed, lodash, will be the only code to appear in your package.json file. This is so other developers can see what top-level projects you need without getting stuck in the details of dependencies.

Here's your updated package.json file. Note that it now has a dependencies field.

architecture/npm/save/package.json

```
{
  "name": "test",
  "version": "1.0.0",
  "description": "",
  "main": "index.js",
  "scripts": {
    "test": "echo \"Error: no test specified\" && exit 1"
  },
  "author": "",
  "license": "ISC",
  "dependencies": {
    "lodash": "^4.17.4"
  }
}
```

Now that you have your code, it's time to use it. Importing the code is simple. You use the same import command from the previous tip, but because you're installing a library, you don't need to give a path.

Here's how you'd import lodash. You can either import an individual function, such as fromPairs(), or you can import the default object. The default lodash import actually contains fromPairs(), but some libraries split things out.

architecture/npm/utils/merge.js

```
import lodash, { fromPairs } from 'lodash';

export function mapToObject(map) {
  return fromPairs([...map]);
}

export function objectToMap(object) {
  const pairs = lodash.toPairs(object);
  return new Map(pairs);
}
```

Looks pretty familiar, huh? The nice part is that no matter where you import the code, you use the same syntax. And when you're reading the code, it's easy to see what functions are from outside the code base. Anything that doesn't use a relative import must be external code.

If npm only tracked dependencies, it would be a great project, but it does more. You'll often need code that does work on the codebase but isn't part of the production build.

For example, you'll want a test runner, but you don't need the test runner to be in your production code. npm will handle the development dependencies *and* give you clean interface for running them.

Say you wanted to add prettier[3] to your project. Prettier is a tool for formatting your code to match style guides. It's a tool for development, not a production dependency.

Because you don't need it in production, you'd install it with the npm install --save-dev prettier flag. Notice that you're using the --save-dev flag. This will also update your package.json file, but it will put the dependency under a different key.

```
architecture/npm/saveDev/package.json
{
  "name": "test",
  "version": "1.0.0",
  "description": "",
  "main": "index.js",
  "scripts": {
    "test": "echo \"Error: no test specified\" && exit 1"
  },
  "author": "",
  "license": "ISC",
  "dependencies": {
    "lodash": "^4.17.4"
  },
  "devDependencies": {
    "prettier": "^1.8.2"
  }
}
```

Of course, now you probably want to use it. Prettier is installed in your node_modules directory, which means you can't access it on the command line directly. Let's say you wanted to make sure all tabs have a width of four spaces. The documentation says you can convert code by running this command: prettier --tab-width=4 --write ./code/*.js.

The command won't work if you installed the code locally. If you installed the package globally—npm install -g prettier—then you'd be able to run the command,

---

3.   https://prettier.io

but then the package wouldn't live specifically in your project. You'd have to somehow communicate to other developers the project has a global dependency.

You can solve the problem using npm scripts. With an npm script, you run the exact same command, but the script looks in the node_modules directory. To run the command, add it to the script object of your package.json file. Change the scripts object to include a key of clean with a value of prettier --tab-width=4 --write./code/*.js.

Now, when you're in the same directory as your package.json file, you can run npm run clean and npm will execute the command using the locally installed prettier package.

architecture/npm/script/package.json

```
{
  "name": "test",
  "version": "1.0.0",
  "description": "",
  "main": "index.js",
  "scripts": {
    "clean": "prettier --tab-width=4 --write ./code/*.js"
  },
  "author": "",
  "license": "ISC",
  "dependencies": {
    "lodash": "^4.17.4"
  },
  "devDependencies": {
    "prettier": "^1.8.2"
  }
}
```

Try it out. Clone the code for this book; then navigate to architecture/npm/script, and run npm install and then npm run clean, and prettier will update the code to have a tab-width of four spaces.

Not only is the dependency scoped to your local project, but other developers can see your build process, dependencies, and package information in a single file.

It's hard to overstate how valuable npm is for JavaScript development. If you ever start looking through a new project, you should begin by skimming the package.json file.

Now that you have the tools to combine multiple files and code from open source projects, it's time to think about how to organize your code.

In the next tip, you'll learn how to organize project assets in a single directory with component architecture.

Tip 49

Build Applications with Component Architecture

In this tip, you'll learn how to gather related HTML, JavaScript, and CSS together using component architecture.

Organizing files can be a challenge. Front-end code—HTML, CSS, Java-Script—can be particularly challenging because the code is made of different languages and file types.

Do you arrange code by file type? What about when CSS is tied to a single HTML file? Do you keep them in different directories but with similar file names?

For a long time, developers would keep files separated by type. The root directory would contain a css directory, a js directory, an img directory, and so on.

Organizing files like this showed good intentions. Everyone wanted to keep different areas of concern separate. The HTML markup (what a site contains) is different from the CSS (how a site looks), which is different from the JavaScript (how a site responds). It seemed like they should be in separate directories.

The problem was that the pieces aren't really separate concerns. Except for a few global styles, CSS is built to work with specific markup. What happens when that markup is removed? If you have disciplined developers, they'd remove the relevant CSS. But most of the time, it stayed. It was never used—it just took up space.

As developer tools improved, a new pattern emerged. The new pattern is component architecture. A component is the combination of all relevant code into a single directory. You then build a web page or application by adding pieces one at a time—a button is in a sidebar, which is in a page—until you have your working application.

Component architecture isn't without problems. The biggest problem with component architecture is that it depends on build tools and, to a lesser extent, frameworks. In this tip, you'll be working with React code. You're going to use scaffolding developed by create-react-app.[4] This means you don't have to worry about setting up the build system. You'll explore that a little in the next tip.

---

4. https://github.com/facebookincubator/create-react-app

It's important to understand, however, that component architecture is not React specific. You can apply the idea in a variety of frameworks. Cody Lindley wrote a great article on the subject.[5] Still, a framework saves some of the trouble of laying a foundation.

To see component architecture at work, build a basic component: a copyright statement. A copyright statement contains the current year, a declaration of copyright, and some styling. With component architecture, you combine everything into a simple package. Here's an example:

architecture/component/simplifying-js-component/src/components/Copyright/Copyright.js

```
import React from 'react';
import './Copyright.css';

export default function CopyrightStatement() {
  const year = new Date().getFullYear();
  return (
    <div className="copyright">
      Copyright {year}
    </div>
  );
}
```

To start off, notice that the markup is in a return statement, and the CSS class is called className. Don't worry about that. The specialized markup is called JSX and it's part of the React framework. You can pretend that the HTML is a separate thing. It effectively is separate. For purposes of this tip, it's just markup that happens to live inside a JavaScript function.

Next, notice the path to the code at the top of the sample. Most of the time, you can ignore it, but in this case, it's relevant. simplifying-js-component is the root of the project. The code lives inside the src/components directory. There's also a public directory that will eventually contain the compiled code. A browser can't handle components, so everything will eventually combine to simpler components.

The components directory contains every component you work with. Each component will then have its own separate directory. In this case, there's a directory called Copyright that contains Copyright.css, Copyright.js, and Copyright.spec.js. The capitalized names are also a React convention.

The Copyright directory contains everything the copyright component will need. If you wanted to share the component, you could put it in a separate repo or just copy and paste it in another project. If you decide you don't want the copyright anymore, you can delete the whole directory. You wouldn't need to worry that dead CSS lives somewhere else. Everything is together.

---

5.   https://developer.telerik.com/featured/front-end-application-frameworks-component-architectures/

Speaking of CSS, notice how this file imports the CSS directly. Because you aren't importing an object from the CSS, you merely include the whole file. The build tools will know what to do with it. The CSS file for this example is very short. All it contains is the font-size, margin, and float.

architecture/component/simplifying-js-component/src/components/Copyright/Copyright.css

```css
.copyright {
    font-size: 10px;
    margin: 1em 1em 1em 0;
    float: left;
}
```

In the JavaScript file, you get the current year and add it to the markup. Notice how simple this is. Everything you need to know about that copyright statement is in a single place. You don't need to guess if the year is calculated or hard coded. It's right there with the markup. You don't need to search for the CSS if you need to change a margin. It's in the same directory.

How about a slightly more complicated component? Think about a button that has an icon. The button will need styling and markup, but it will also need the image asset and a click action.

This time, you also want to make the component reusable. That means you should hard code as few options as you can. Don't explicitly say what happens on click. Instead, inject the click action into a component. Passing in actions or assets to a component is another form of dependency injection that you explored in Tip 32, *Write Functions for Testability*, on page 151. It keeps things flexible and reusable.

architecture/component/simplifying-js-component/src/components/IdeaButton/IdeaButton.js

```js
import React from 'react';
import './IdeaButton.css';
import idea from './idea.svg';

export default function IdeaButton({ handleClick, message }) {
  return (
    <button
      className="idea-button"
      onClick={handleClick}
    >
      <img
        className="idea-button__icon"
        src={idea}
        alt="idea icon"
      />
      { message }
    </button>
  );
}
```

In React, you can access the injected dependencies in the arguments of a function. And you can pull them apart using destructuring. The message will change depending on what's injected. The curly braces are a templating language, and they surround variable information. In other words, the button will contain the value of the message variable.

Notice also that you're importing an image. Unlike when you import the CSS without ever using it, in this case, you're importing the image to a variable. The variable contains the path of the image, so set the src to the variable using the curly braces.

Now that you have the pieces, you can start building a page. In this case, the page is just another component! This page will contain the idea button and the copyright notice in a footer. You're still in React territory, so you inject the message as a special HTML attribute. Other frameworks use different conventions to inject data. But they all allow you to pass in some information—this is what makes components so powerful.

architecture/component/simplifying-js-component/src/App.js

```
import React from 'react';

import './App.css';
import IdeaButton from './components/IdeaButton/IdeaButton';
import Copyright from './components/Copyright/Copyright';

function logIdea() {
  console.log('Someone had an idea!');
}
export default function App() {
  return (
    <div className="main">
      <div className="app">
        <IdeaButton
          message="I have an idea!"
          handleClick={logIdea}
        />
      </div>
      <footer>
        <Copyright />
        <IdeaButton
          message="Footer idea!"
          handleClick={logIdea}
        />
      </footer>
    </div>
  );
}
```

Because App.js is the main component, it lives at the root of the source code. Otherwise, it's the same. It imports code, it contains all the pieces, and it combines them together. In this case, you're reusing the button component twice. Each one will have a different message. As you can see in the following figure, the result isn't stunning, but it does show each piece.

Download the source code and try it out. The code contains a README.md, which will get you up and running with only two commands. After that, try changing some CSS. Try adding a new image. You'll see how simple it is to work with components when everything is in one logical place.

If you inspected the page, you'd notice something interesting. You combined the separate CSS files into a single file and moved that file to a separate css directory. The same thing happened to images. In this case, the build tools still separate out the pieces into different directories. That's great! There's nothing wrong with having pieces separate at the user level. The goal is to make development easier.

Intuitively, component architecture probably makes sense. Keep like things together. The only downside is that wiring everything together isn't easy. The only reason component architecture works is because you can use great tools that intelligently combine code.

In the next tip, you'll learn how to compile front-end code with build tools.

Tip 50

Use Build Tools to Combine Components

In this tip, you'll learn how to compile JavaScript code and assets with build tools.

In the previous tip, you saw the advantages of the component architecture. You also learned about the one big problem with component architecture: It won't work natively in browsers.

Also in the previous tip, you used the tools provided by create-react-app[6] to get your project compiled and running. That's great. You should always take advantage of predesigned build tools. Every project has one. Sometimes there are official projects—angular-cli and EmberCLI are examples—and if there are no official projects, search code repos such as github for Starter Packs. Eventually, however, you'll need to customize your build.

In this tip, you're going to make a basic build process. Build tools can be exhausting, and it can be difficult to keep up with the latest trends and tools. Don't get discouraged. A build tool is merely a way for you to process the code one piece at a time.

To begin, take a simplified version of your components from the previous tip. Start by removing everything except for some HTML, in the form of React JSX, and some JavaScript. It'll be easier to make build tools when you have fewer assets. Here's a basic container component:

architecture/build/initial/src/App.js
```
import React from 'react';

import Copyright from './components/Copyright/Copyright';

export default function App() {
  return (
    <div className="main">
      <footer>
        <Copyright />
      </footer>
    </div>
  );
}
```

---

6.   https://github.com/facebookincubator/create-react-app

Here's a stripped down version of your copyright component:

architecture/build/initial/src/components/Copyright/Copyright.js
```
import React from 'react';

export default function CopyrightStatement() {
  const year = new Date().getFullYear();
  return (
    <div className="copyright">
      Copyright {year}
    </div>
  );
}
```

Even though these files are simple, you couldn't run them in a browser. And even if you could, you certainly wouldn't be able to run them in older browsers. You need a tool to convert ES6 syntax—import and export— and JSX into compatible code.

Fortunately, there's an amazing tool called Babel[7] that can convert bleeding-edge JavaScript to browser-friendly code. Babel is the single-most important tool you have for working with modern JavaScript. Not only does it convert your ES6+ JavaScript, but you can even configure Babel to use syntax that's still in committee.

To get started, you need to install the Babel command-line interface (cli) along with the preset-env to convert ES6+ and babel-present-react to convert react code.

The installation command should look familiar. This time, you're installing three packages with a single command.

```
npm install --save-dev babel-cli babel-preset-env babel-preset-react
```

The next thing you need to do is set up a .babelrc file to hold your configuration information. This file tells Babel what kind of code you have and how Babel will need to convert it. In this case, you have ES6 code—signified with env—and react code.

architecture/build/initial/.babelrc
```
{ "presets": ["env", "react"] }
```

Now add a script to your package.json file and you'll be ready to compile. Notice that you're outputting the compiled information to a single file, bundle.js, in the build directory. Here's your final package.json.

---

7.   https://babeljs.io/

architecture/build/initial/package.json

```
{
  "name": "initial",
  "version": "1.0.0",
  "description": "",
  "main": "index.js",
  "scripts": {
    "build": "babel src/index.js -o build/bundle.js"
  },
  "keywords": [],
  "author": "",
  "license": "ISC",
  "devDependencies": {
    "babel-cli": "^6.26.0",
    "babel-preset-env": "^1.6.1",
    "babel-preset-react": "^6.24.1"
  },
  "dependencies": {
    "react": "^16.1.1",
    "react-dom": "^16.1.1"
  }
}
```

Finally, update your index.html to use the compiled code:

architecture/build/initial/index.html

```
<!DOCTYPE html>
<html lang="en">
  <head>
    <title>Sample</title>
  </head>
  <body>
    <div id="root">
    </div>
    <script src="./build/bundle.js"></script>
  </body>
</html>
```

If you try to open that file in a browser, you'll encounter a problem. The console will display an error: Uncaught ReferenceError: require isn't defined.

Babel converts the code, but it doesn't include a module loader, which handles the compiled imports and exports. You have a few options for module loaders. Currently, the most popular module loaders are webpack[8] and rollup.js.[9] In this example, you'll use webpack.

---

8.   https://webpack.js.org
9.   https://rollupjs.org/

Webpack is a project that can handle everything from combining your Java-Script, to processing your CSS or SASS, to image conversion. Webpack can handle so many file types because you declare different actions—referred to as loaders in webpack—based on file extension.

To get webpack working, you'll need to install it. You'll also need to install a loader for Babel. The webpack documentation encourages you to think of loaders as a task in another build tool.[10] Because compiling the code with Babel is just a step in getting usable JavaScript, you'll need the babel-loader. You can install them both in the same command: npm install --save-dev babel-loader webpack.

You'll also need to create a webpack.config.js file. Inside the file, declare an entry point and an output path. After that, you need to tell webpack what to do with the code it encounters. This is where the loaders come in.

At this point, you're probably getting overwhelmed. So remember: Don't think of the whole system—just think about each step. You first needed to convert ES6 and React code, so you installed Babel. Next, you wanted to combine everything together, so you installed webpack. Now, you need to declare what you want webpack to do with JavaScript specifically. Next, you'll make similar declarations for style and assets.

Webpack uses regular expressions to decide which loader to use on each file. Because you're working with JavaScript, you only want files that match .js. When webpack encounters a file with a .js extension—such as Copyright.js—you need to tell it which loader to use. In this case, it needs to run the babel-loader.

architecture/build/webpack/webpack.config.js
```
const path = require('path');

module.exports = {
  entry: './src/index.js',
  module: {
    loaders: [
      {
        test: /\.js?/,
        use: 'babel-loader',
      },
    ],
  },
  output: {
    filename: 'build/bundle.js',
    path: path.resolve(__dirname),
  },
};
```

---

10. https://webpack.js.org/concepts/#loaders

The last step is to update your package.json script to call webpack. Webpack will look for your config file, so you don't need any other flags or arguments. All you need to do is change

```
"scripts": {
  "build": "babel src/index.js -o build/bundle.js"
}
```

to:

```
"scripts": {
  "build": "webpack"
}
```

If you run this, you'll finally be able to see your code in the browser. Try it out.

Now that you have the JavaScript working, it's time for things to get interesting. Remember, the goal is to have components that import all their dependencies. You need webpack to compile your JavaScript, but also to compile your CSS and load your images.

Start with CSS. Go back to your Copyright.js file and import your CSS. It should look exactly like it did in the previous tip.

architecture/build/css/src/components/Copyright/Copyright.js
```
import React from 'react';
import './Copyright.css';

export default function CopyrightStatement() {
  const year = new Date().getFullYear();
  return (
    <div className="copyright">
      Copyright {year}
    </div>
  );
}
```

Now you'll need to install a CSS loader and update your webpack.config.js file. There are lots of tools for handling CSS, but in this case, keep it simple. Install and add two loaders—a CSS loader to interpret the CSS file and a style loader to inject the styles into the <head> element on your page.

npm install --save-dev css-loader style-loader.

Now that you've installed your loaders, update your webpack config by adding a test for files that end in css. This time, you won't use a single loader. You'll use two loaders—css-loader and style-loader—so you'll need an array of strings instead of a single string. Add the style-loader first and then the css-loader.

architecture/build/css/webpack.config.js
```
module: {
  loaders: [
    {
      test: /\.css$/,
      use: [
        'style-loader',
        'css-loader',
      ],
    },
    {
      test: /\.js?/,
      use: 'babel-loader',
    },
  ],
},
```

When you run the build script and open index.html, your components will have the correct styles.

Impressive, huh? This is why developers fell in love with webpack. You can keep all your assets batched together and you can call different actions, or series of actions, on each file type.

The final step is to handle your image. This time you aren't compiling an image. Instead, you're going to use webpack to move the file and rename it to a unique name. Webpack will automatically update the src link in your markup.

As a reminder, here's your component with an imported image:

architecture/build/img/src/components/IdeaButton/IdeaButton.js
```
import React from 'react';
import './IdeaButton.css';
import idea from './idea.svg';

export default function IdeaButton({ handleClick, message }) {
  return (
    <button
      className="idea-button"
      onClick={handleClick}
    >
      <img
        className="idea-button__icon"
        src={idea}
        alt="idea icon"
      />
      { message }
    </button>
  );
}
```

Because you aren't doing any specific image manipulation, use file-loader to move and update your src path. In your webpack config, you'll test to see if the file is an SVG.

This time, you aren't just declaring a loader; you're also passing options to the loader. This means you'll pass an array containing a single object. The object will include your loader and configuration options. The only option you need to pass is the directory for your images. This directory will be where the browser looks for images, so it's best to reuse your build directory.

Set the outputPath to the build directory:

architecture/build/img/webpack.config.js
```
module: {
  loaders: [
    {
      test: /\.svg?/,
      use: [
        {
          loader: 'file-loader',
          options: {
            outputPath: 'build/',
          },
        },
      ],
    },
    {
      test: /\.css$/,
      use: [
        'style-loader',
        'css-loader',
      ],
    },
    {
      test: /\.js?/,
      use: 'babel-loader',
    },
  ],
},
```

Run the build script. Open up index.html and you have your components.

See that wasn't so bad! Of course, if this were an enterprise application, you'd want a server. You'll probably have more images than just SVGs. You might want the CSS to go to a style sheet instead of <style> tags. Build tools can handle all that for you.

The key is to take it slow and add one piece at a time. It's much harder to add a configuration to a large project than it is to add it piece by piece. Webpack and rollup.js can be complex projects. Webpack has put a lot of work into updating its documentation,[11] and it's worth reading as you explore more on your own.

At this point, you have all the tools you need to write modern JavaScript applications. The final tip is a little different. CSS and HTML are also growing and evolving—actions that used to require JavaScript can now be handled by CSS. In this case, you should happily abandon JavaScript and use other tools.

In the next tip, you'll see how to animate page elements with CSS.

---

11. https://webpack.js.org/concepts/

Leverage CSS for Animations

In this tip, you'll learn how to use CSS for animations.

The last tip isn't even a JavaScript tip. Instead, it's a tip about when to stop using JavaScript.

The key to writing readable code is to use the best tool for the job. JavaScript used to be the best tool for animations. In fact, there were entire libraries dedicated to using JavaScript to create drop-down menus or to animate slide-in elements.

It's much easier now. CSS is replacing JavaScript for simple animations. That's great. Now you don't have to worry about using the right timeouts or calculating odd-size constraints. CSS will take care of all that for you. You'll still need JavaScript for more complicated animations, but for most common tasks, CSS works great.

Start by creating a simple page that has a menu on the right. The markup is very simple. You need some text, a button to toggle the side menu, and the menu itself.

architecture/css/initial/index-truncated.html
```html
<!doctype html>
<html lang="en">
    <head>
        <link href="main.css" rel="stylesheet">
    </head>
    <body>
        <div class="main">
            <h1>Moby Dick</h1>
            <button id="show">See More</button>
            <section class="menu" id="sidebar">
                <h2>Other Works</h2>
                <ul>
                    <li>Bartleby, the Scrivener</li>
                    <li>Billy Budd</li>
                </ul>
            </section>
            <section class="content">
                <p>
                    Call me Ishmael.
                    <!-- More content -->
```

```
                </p>
            </section>
        </div>
    </body>
</html>
```

Start with simple CSS to place the menu on top of the text.

architecture/css/initial/main.css

```
.main {
    width: 1000px;
    margin: 0 auto;
    overflow: hidden;
    position: relative;
}
button {
    border: black solid 1px;
    background: #ffffff;
}

.menu {
    width: 300px;
    padding: 0 2em;
    float: right;
    border: black solid 1px;
    position: absolute;
    top: 0;
    right: 0;
    height: calc(100% - 2px);
    background: #ffffff;
}
```

As you see in the figure on page 250, when the menu is fully opened, it will cover a portion of the words. You'll change that in a moment.

Now that you have the page set up, you're going to add some CSS animations to slide the menu on and off the page.

The first step is hiding the side menu. Add the following property to your .menu class.

transform: translateX(calc(300px + 4em + 2px));

This property and value—transform: translateX—will move the page outside the container div, making it appear invisible. The calculation is the width of the menu, plus the padding, plus the border.

With the menu hidden, it's time to add a transition. A CSS transition is an animation of a changing property. In other words, an animation is just a visual transition between two properties of the same name.

Moby Dick

See More

Call me Ishmael. Some years ago—never mind how long precisely—having little or no money in m
thought I would sail about a little and see the watery part of the world. It is a way I have of driving
find myself growing grim about the mouth; whenever it is a damp, drizzly November in my soul; w
warehouses, and bringing up the rear of every funeral I meet; and especially whenever my hypos g
moral principle to prevent me from deliberately stepping into the street, and methodically knocking
sea as soon as I can. This is my substitute for pistol and ball. With a philosophical flourish Cato thr
There is nothing surprising in this. If they but knew it, almost all men in their degree, some time or
ocean with me.

There now is your insular city of the Manhattoes, belted round by wharves as Indian isles by coral
left, the streets take you waterward. Its extreme downtown is the battery, where that noble mole is
hours previous were out of sight of land. Look at the crowds of water-gazers there.

Circumambulate the city of a dreamy Sabbath afternoon. Go from Corlears Hook to Coenties Slip,
see?—Posted like silent sentinels all around the town, stand thousands upon thousands of mortal m
spiles; some seated upon the pier-heads; some looking over the bulwarks of ships from China; som
better seaward peep. But these are all landsmen; of week days pent up in lath and plaster—tied to c
is this? Are the green fields gone? What do they here?

But look! here come more crowds, pacing straight for the water, and seemingly bound for a dive. S
of the land; loitering under the shady lee of yonder warehouses will not suffice. No. They must get
falling in. And there they stand—miles of them—leagues. Inlanders all, they come from lanes and
Yet here they all unite. Tell me, does the magnetic virtue of the needles of the compasses of all thos

Once more. Say you are in the country; in some high land of lakes. Take almost any path you pleas
you there by a pool in the stream. There is magic in it. Let the most absent-minded of men be plung
set his feet a-going, and he will infallibly lead you to water, if water there be in all that region. Sho
this experiment, if your caravan happen to be supplied with a metaphysical professor. Yes, as every

Other Works

- Bartleby, the Scrivener
- Billy Budd

That's fine, but how do you change a property? Turns out, you'll need a little JavaScript after all. Add a click event listener to the button. The callback function for the button will toggle the .display class on the menu. The first time you click the button, it will add the class. The second time you click the button, it will remove the class.

architecture/css/middle/open.js
```
const sidebar = document.getElementById('sidebar');
document.getElementById('show')
  .addEventListener('click', () => {
    sidebar.classList.toggle('display');
  });
```

Next, you need to update your stylesheet to include styles for a .menu.display

architecture/css/middle/main.css
```
.menu {
    /* Other styles from before */
    transform: translateX(calc(300px + 4em +  2px));
}
.menu.display {
    transform: translateX(0);
}
```

When you add the class, you move from a transform of calc(300px + 4em + 2px) to a transform of 0. Because the browser knows that property is changing, it can trigger an animation. All that's left is to tell the element how to respond to the changing property.

A CSS transition is a set of instructions telling the page what to do when moving from an initial property value to the final property value. Check out the Mozilla Developer Network documentation for different options.[12]

First, declare the property that will need a transition with transition-property. In this case, you only want to animate the transform, so set the value to transform. Next, set the length of the durations with transition-duration.

The transition time will seem very quick or very slow depending on how radical the transition is. Going from 0px to 10px in one second will seem much slower than going from 0 to 100px. In this case, set it for 600ms.

Finally, you need to say how the transition should act with the transition-timing-function property. This one is a little more tricky. It can make the transition move faster at the beginning, faster at the ending, or the same speed throughout.[13] Set the value to linear to keep a nice smooth slide throughout.

Here's the updated CSS for .menu.display:

```
architecture/css/animate/main.css
.menu.display {
    /* Other styles */
    transform: translateX(0);
    transition-property: transform;
    transition-duration: 600ms;
    transition-timing-function: linear;
}
```

When you click the button, you should see the menu slide into place. But when you click it again, the menu will just instantly disappear. The problem is that you only declared the transition for when you add the .display class. There's no transition for when you remove the .display.

No problem—all you need to do is add a transition to the base .menu styles. This time, though, you can shorten things up. You can add all three properties—transition-property, transition-duration, and transition-timing-function—to a single property called transition. You also have the option to apply the transition to *any* changing property by setting the transition to all.

Once you update the stylesheet, you'll have a menu that slides in on button click and slides out on button click with very minimal JavaScript.

---

12. https://developer.mozilla.org/en-US/docs/Web/CSS/CSS_Transitions/Using_CSS_transitions
13. https://developer.mozilla.org/en-US/docs/Web/CSS/transition-timing-function

architecture/css/animate/main.css
```
.menu {
    /* Other styles */
    transform: translateX(calc(300px + 4em +  2px));
    transition: all 600ms linear;
}
```

Honestly, you only need the transition on the .menu class, unless you want the slide in and slide out to be different. Transitions are like any other property. They'll bubble up to all elements unless you override them with a more specific selector.

This simple slide-in used to require a lot of JavaScript code. Now it only takes a single line of CSS and a simple class toggle. Part of what makes web development such a delight is the tool set is steadily improving. HTML is more semantic. Styles are more flexible. JavaScript is simpler and easier to read.

JavaScript is a great language, and I hope you learned to love it. It's simple, expressive, and very elegant. And the best part is it's getting better all the time. You have everything you need to start writing JavaScript that you can be proud of. Now all you need to do is start building. Have fun.

Bibliography

[Fog13]   Michael Fogus. *Functional JavaScript*. O'Reilly & Associates, Inc., Sebastopol, CA, 2013.

[Sim14]   Kyle Simpson. *You Don't Know JS: this Object Prototypes*. O'Reilly & Associates, Inc., Sebastopol, CA, 2014.

[Sub16]   Venkat Subramaniam. *Test-Driving JavaScript Applications*. The Pragmatic Bookshelf, Raleigh, NC, 2016.

Index

Thank you!

How did you enjoy this book? Please let us know. Take a moment and email us at support@pragprog.com with your feedback. Tell us your story and you could win free ebooks. Please use the subject line "Book Feedback."

Ready for your next great Pragmatic Bookshelf book? Come on over to https://pragprog.com and use the coupon code BUYANOTHER2018 to save 30% on your next ebook.

Void where prohibited, restricted, or otherwise unwelcome. Do not use ebooks near water. If rash persists, see a doctor. Doesn't apply to *The Pragmatic Programmer* ebook because it's older than the Pragmatic Bookshelf itself. Side effects may include increased knowledge and skill, increased marketability, and deep satisfaction. Increase dosage regularly.

And thank you for your continued support,

Andy Hunt, Publisher

Pragmatic Bookshelf

SAVE 30%!
Use coupon code
BUYANOTHER2018

Secure JavaScript and Web Testing

Secure your Node applications and see how to really test on the web.

Secure Your Node.js Web Application

Cyber-criminals have your web applications in their crosshairs. They search for and exploit common security mistakes in your web application to steal user data. Learn how you can secure your Node.js applications, database and web server to avoid these security holes. Discover the primary attack vectors against web applications, and implement security best practices and effective countermeasures. Coding securely will make you a stronger web developer and analyst, and you'll protect your users.

Karl Düüna
(230 pages) ISBN: 9781680500851. $36
https://pragprog.com/book/kdnodesec

The Way of the Web Tester

This book is for everyone who needs to test the web. As a tester, you'll automate your tests. As a developer, you'll build more robust solutions. And as a team, you'll gain a vocabulary and a means to coordinate how to write and organize automated tests for the web. Follow the testing pyramid and level up your skills in user interface testing, integration testing, and unit testing. Your new skills will free you up to do other, more important things while letting the computer do the one thing it's really good at: quickly running thousands of repetitive tasks.

Jonathan Rasmusson
(256 pages) ISBN: 9781680501834. $29
https://pragprog.com/book/jrtest

Level Up

From data structures to architecture and design, we have what you need.

A Common-Sense Guide to Data Structures and Algorithms

If you last saw algorithms in a university course or at a job interview, you're missing out on what they can do for your code. Learn different sorting and searching techniques, and when to use each. Find out how to use recursion effectively. Discover structures for specialized applications, such as trees and graphs. Use Big O notation to decide which algorithms are best for your production environment. Beginners will learn how to use these techniques from the start, and experienced developers will rediscover approaches they may have forgotten.

Jay Wengrow
(218 pages) ISBN: 9781680502442. $45.95
https://pragprog.com/book/jwdsal

Design It!

Don't engineer by coincidence—design it like you mean it! Grounded by fundamentals and filled with practical design methods, this is the perfect introduction to software architecture for programmers who are ready to grow their design skills. Ask the right stakeholders the right questions, explore design options, share your design decisions, and facilitate collaborative workshops that are fast, effective, and fun. Become a better programmer, leader, and designer. Use your new skills to lead your team in implementing software with the right capabilities—and develop awesome software!

Michael Keeling
(358 pages) ISBN: 9781680502091. $41.95
https://pragprog.com/book/mkdsa

Long Live the Command Line!

Use tmux and Vim for incredible mouse-free productivity.

tmux 2

Your mouse is slowing you down. The time you spend context switching between your editor and your consoles eats away at your productivity. Take control of your environment with tmux, a terminal multiplexer that you can tailor to your workflow. With this updated second edition for tmux 2.3, you'll customize, script, and leverage tmux's unique abilities to craft a productive terminal environment that lets you keep your fingers on your keyboard's home row.

Brian P. Hogan
(102 pages) ISBN: 9781680502213. $21.95
https://pragprog.com/book/bhtmux2

Modern Vim

Turn Vim into a full-blown development environment using Vim 8's new features and this sequel to the beloved bestseller *Practical Vim*. Integrate your editor with tools for building, testing, linting, indexing, and searching your codebase. Discover the future of Vim with Neovim: a fork of Vim that includes a built-in terminal emulator that will transform your workflow. Whether you choose to switch to Neovim or stick with Vim 8, you'll be a better developer.

Drew Neil
(190 pages) ISBN: 9781680502626. $39.95
https://pragprog.com/book/modvim

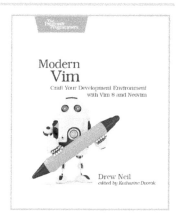

Fix Your Hidden Problems

From technical debt to deployment in the very real, very messy world, we've got the tools you need to fix the hidden problems before they become disasters.

Software Design X-Rays

Are you working on a codebase where cost overruns, death marches, and heroic fights with legacy code monsters are the norm? Battle these adversaries with novel ways to identify and prioritize technical debt, based on behavioral data from how developers work with code. And that's just for starters. Because good code involves social design, as well as technical design, you can find surprising dependencies between people and code to resolve coordination bottlenecks among teams. Best of all, the techniques build on behavioral data that you already have: your version-control system. Join the fight for better code!

Adam Tornhill
(274 pages) ISBN: 9781680502725. $45.95
https://pragprog.com/book/atevol

Release It! Second Edition

A single dramatic software failure can cost a company millions of dollars—but can be avoided with simple changes to design and architecture. This new edition of the best-selling industry standard shows you how to create systems that run longer, with fewer failures, and recover better when bad things happen. New coverage includes DevOps, microservices, and cloud-native architecture. Stability antipatterns have grown to include systemic problems in large-scale systems. This is a must-have pragmatic guide to engineering for production systems.

Michael Nygard
(376 pages) ISBN: 9781680502398. $47.95
https://pragprog.com/book/mnee2

Python for All

For data science and basic science, for you and anyone else on your team.

Data Science Essentials in Python

Go from messy, unstructured artifacts stored in SQL and NoSQL databases to a neat, well-organized dataset with this quick reference for the busy data scientist. Understand text mining, machine learning, and network analysis; process numeric data with the NumPy and Pandas modules; describe and analyze data using statistical and network-theoretical methods; and see actual examples of data analysis at work. This one-stop solution covers the essential data science you need in Python.

Dmitry Zinoviev
(224 pages) ISBN: 9781680501841. $29
https://pragprog.com/book/dzpyds

Practical Programming, Third Edition

Classroom-tested by tens of thousands of students, this new edition of the best-selling intro to programming book is for anyone who wants to understand computer science. Learn about design, algorithms, testing, and debugging. Discover the fundamentals of programming with Python 3.6—a language that's used in millions of devices. Write programs to solve real-world problems, and come away with everything you need to produce quality code. This edition has been updated to use the new language features in Python 3.6.

Paul Gries, Jennifer Campbell, Jason Montojo
(410 pages) ISBN: 9781680502688. $49.95
https://pragprog.com/book/gwpy3

A Better Web with Phoenix and Elm

Elixir and Phoenix on the server side with Elm on the front end gets you the best of both worlds in both worlds!

Functional Web Development with Elixir, OTP, and Phoenix

Elixir and Phoenix are generating tremendous excitement as an unbeatable platform for building modern web applications. For decades OTP has helped developers create incredibly robust, scalable applications with unparalleled uptime. Make the most of them as you build a stateful web app with Elixir, OTP, and Phoenix. Model domain entities without an ORM or a database. Manage server state and keep your code clean with OTP Behaviours. Layer on a Phoenix web interface without coupling it to the business logic. Open doors to powerful new techniques that will get you thinking about web development in fundamentally new ways.

Lance Halvorsen
(218 pages) ISBN: 9781680502435. $45.95
https://pragprog.com/book/lhelph

Programming Elm

Elm brings the safety and stability of functional programing to front-end development, making it one of the most popular new languages. Elm's functional nature and static typing means that run-time errors are nearly impossible, and it compiles to JavaScript for easy web deployment. This book helps you take advantage of this new language in your web site development. Learn how the Elm Architecture will help you create fast applications. Discover how to integrate Elm with JavaScript so you can update legacy applications. See how Elm tooling makes deployment quicker and easier.

Jeremy Fairbank
(250 pages) ISBN: 9781680502855. $40.95
https://pragprog.com/book/jfelm

The Pragmatic Bookshelf

The Pragmatic Bookshelf features books written by developers for developers. The titles continue the well-known Pragmatic Programmer style and continue to garner awards and rave reviews. As development gets more and more difficult, the Pragmatic Programmers will be there with more titles and products to help you stay on top of your game.

Visit Us Online

This Book's Home Page
https://pragprog.com/book/es6tips
Source code from this book, errata, and other resources. Come give us feedback, too!

Register for Updates
https://pragprog.com/updates
Be notified when updates and new books become available.

Join the Community
https://pragprog.com/community
Read our weblogs, join our online discussions, participate in our mailing list, interact with our wiki, and benefit from the experience of other Pragmatic Programmers.

New and Noteworthy
https://pragprog.com/news
Check out the latest pragmatic developments, new titles and other offerings.

Save on the eBook

Save on the eBook versions of this title. Owning the paper version of this book entitles you to purchase the electronic versions at a terrific discount.

PDFs are great for carrying around on your laptop—they are hyperlinked, have color, and are fully searchable. Most titles are also available for the iPhone and iPod touch, Amazon Kindle, and other popular e-book readers.

Buy now at *https://pragprog.com/coupon*

Contact Us

Online Orders:	*https://pragprog.com/catalog*
Customer Service:	*support@pragprog.com*
International Rights:	*translations@pragprog.com*
Academic Use:	*academic@pragprog.com*
Write for Us:	*http://write-for-us.pragprog.com*
Or Call:	+1 800-699-7764

Milton Keynes UK
Ingram Content Group UK Ltd.
UKHW012338190824
447149UK00007B/133